Female Bigfoot

Encounters

Names and places have been changed to protect people and properties. This story has been vetted for truth and authenticity.

Before you begin, please let me remind you that I am an Independent Author. I create my books. They are all written in General Casual. If you find the occasional Typo. I apologize. I don't have a group of people sitting in their office waiting to go over my book before it reaches you. The English used in the majority of my books may not be proper at times. This is better to convey the story to you, as it was told to me without sounding like a textbook. With this being said, I hope you enjoy this book cover to cover. If you do, please think about leaving me a review. Your reviews can make or break an independent author. If you didn't care for the book. I understand. We can't connect with every book. Just try to go easy on me in your review. Thank you.

To whom it may concern, the thoughts, opinions, and beliefs of the ones that submitted their stories for the content of this book are not necessarily the thoughts, opinions, and views of Melissa George, Cari George and/or Tye Chapman. These stories were all submitted on the grounds of being true. However, we have no way of verifying all of these encounters, so we ask that you read with an open mind and open heart. Sometimes. It's not easy to put your story out there for the public to ridicule and scrutinize. We want to thank every woman that took the time to send us her story.

This book in no way reflects on The Carolina Cryptid Crew, it's members, or their beliefs.

I have noticed in the past few years, there have begun to be more and more Female Bigfoot Hunters. I am thrilled to see this. But on the flip side, it is still mostly the men that are getting credit. The majority of online groups and blogs are run by men. Don't get me wrong, there isn't a problem with this. We would just like to see the women come forward and start taking more of an active role in our community. And for those that have, I send a round of applause!

I have talked to a lot of women that say, "I don't want to be out in the woods and come across an eight-foot monster!" The chances of that happening are actually pretty slim. Bigfoot Hunting / Tracking / Research is basically about gathering all of the evidence you possibly can and keeping well-documented notes. You want to find a place that we like to call, "A Bigfoot Hotspot." Somewhere that there have been some reported sightings. Get out there and spend a day familiarizing yourself with the terrain and the lay of the land. We like to use Google maps and check a place out before we ever get out there on foot. You can look for evidence your first day out. Look for prints and tree structures. Anything that doesn't look natural. Familiarize yourself with the sounds. If you find anything at all, please make notes. Note what was found and where, note the date, the time of day, the weather. I can't stress enough that keeping records on your finds is highly essential. Eventually, with well-kept notes, you will begin to see a pattern emerge.

I want to encourage you to hit the woods!

You will find that being out in the woods brings about peace and tranquility. A slow walk through nature can rejuvenate the mind and spirit, not to mention that you are getting some exercise to boot. And who knows, you may end up being the one that proves the existence of Bigfoot!

The stories contained within this book are the property of the original owner. We have accepted many stories from many people. There is no way for us to verify if the stories are true or not, so we ask that you read with an open mind, while giving credit to the original author for coming forward with their account.

(Sometimes, coming forward is not an easy thing to do.)

I'm going to start off by introducing myself and the other Authors and tell you a bit about how we all got started on the quest to find Bigfoot.

My name is Melissa,

my family and friends call me Lisa. I am a

South Carolina native with one grown son, a daughter in law and two small grandchildren.

A few years ago, my family and I joined a paranormal team. After being on this team for a while, we became board members. At one of our meetings, we discussed how some of the newer members had an interest in Cryptids. We wanted to keep all members happy and interested, so we decided to try and branch out a little in the Cryptid direction. Now at the time, none of us knew how this was going to work. We just had an idea that we were going to try. My family and I live out in the country. The majority of the team was in town, we thought we could use our property to get them out in the woods and give them some kind of idea on how we could conduct a Cryptid Investigation (Or expedition).

My father owns a lot of land that is mostly covered with thick woods. There is a creek that runs through the lower part that leads into a pretty large swamp area. We were thinking this would be an excellent area to do some training. We spent some time learning all we could about the known Cryptid's and how to conduct a Cryptid Investigation. As Spring turned into Summer, we were getting ready to get the team out in the woods.

We decided that before bringing the team out that we would need to go check out the woods and find the best areas to move them through. We had a few members that we knew wouldn't be up for a hard hike. With this in mind, we would scout out the woods and find the best route possible

My husband, Marty, and I, along with our son Chris and our DIL, Cari, headed out to the woods. We had walked in a long way when we came across a clearing. The ground here looked somewhat washed away by the rain as there was nothing but red South Carolina clay. We decided this would be a good spot to look and see if there were any kind of animal prints.

Our woods contain a large variety of wildlife. Everything from Raccoon, Possums, white-tailed deer, Wild Boar, Coyote the occasional red fox down to wild turkeys and ducks. We thought if we could photograph some animal prints, we could show the others what was common in our area.

The four of us walked around this area very slowly, looking down at the ground. And being very careful where we placed our feet. We didn't want to run the risk of messing up any prints. We were all a few feet apart, walking around slowly and looking down. I glanced at something that appeared to be the back end of an animal print, as I looked closer, I realized that this was a large print.

My eyes scanned up, and it took a second to register that this print had five toes! I was looking at an impression that was much too big to be created by a human, yet it looked just like a substantial human print. I stood there, taking this in and wondering just how anyone could have gotten out here in their bare feet. It was a very wooded area with a lot of undergrowth. No doubt, they would have had to walk through saw briers and a whole host of unpleasant things that would make walking barefoot impossible.

I called the others over to see if they found this as strange as I did. Naturally, they were all just as shocked as I was. We discussed how there was just no way anyone could have left this print out here, and besides, there was only one print.

I don't remember now just who it was that mentioned Bigfoot first. But it seems that my world stopped spinning for a few seconds. I had never even thought about Bigfoot and wasn't sure I liked this new theory. I immediately scanned the woods around us. Was this thing standing somewhere in the dark shadows watching us? Then I was mesmerized to think that one of these creatures may have walked precisely where I was standing.

The tiny hairs on the back of my neck stood up, and I was sure we were being watched.

I mentally scolded myself for this. We didn't even know what kind of footprint this was. I was jumping to conclusions and scaring myself.

After searching for a while, we did find the second print. It was just at the edge of the clearing. Actually, the heel was the only visible part of this print. It had stepped off the clearing into the undergrowth. And this thing had about a five-foot stride. It had to have been tremendous!

Chris volunteered to walk back and find a tape measure so we could measure the print. (Sixteen inches long with five inches across.) I was fascinated and frightened all at the same time. It had never crossed my mind that we might actually find something out here. I was in awe that I was standing where one of these creatures could have walked, yet I was terrified to think that they could be in these very woods. I was flooded with a lot of emotions all at the same time. My brain hadn't had time to digest this information.

Naturally, I snapped off a few dozen pictures. Then we went back to get the stuff to try casting this large print.

Little did I know that this was just the beginning of our Bigfoot experiences.

My name is Tye,

I was born and raised in Indiana but moved to Iowa in march of twenty fifteen. I am the mother of two and a grandmother of two. At the age of twelve, I saw a movie at the local theater that began my fascination with Sasquatch.

 The movie was The Legend of Boggy Creek. Ever since then, I have been on a quest to find this amazing creature. Since moving to Iowa, I have had extraordinary experiences, from seeing the big guys to hearing them yelling. As long as I live, squatching will be my way of life and hopefully someday being able to prove their existence. Until then, I'll just keep doing what I love, squatching!

My name is Cari,

For the vast majority of my life, I have been interested in Bigfoot. This twenty-three-year journey started when I was barely nine years old and has remained a constant fascination of mine.

In the fourth grade, I was somewhat new to the school but had already gotten to know the school librarian pretty well. Not only did I visit with my class, but it was common to see me on Friday afternoon looking for something to read over the weekend. I felt as if I had read everything the school had to offer. One Friday afternoon, browsing the shelves of my school library, I was getting more and more irritated because I couldn't find anything.

It was going to be the weekend, and I did not want to get stuck with nothing to read. The librarian got my attention and called me to the desk. She informed me that a new book had come in and thought I would be interested.

This book had a strange creature on the front and had something called Bigfoot in the title. This was my first glimpse of Patty, and I was hooked. I went home excited and could not wait to tell my mom about this new animal I learned about. From that day on, I would read anything I could get my hands on and sometimes got lucky with something on television to watch about these amazing mysterious beings.

For the first few years, my mom encouraged this hobby, after all, I was reading. She did discourage my reading of tabloids in the grocery store lines that read "I Had Bigfoot's Baby," or something similar. After her own encounter, which I did not know about at the time, she tried to get me interested in something new, but my fascination never stopped.

I have always had my own theories about Bigfoot- maybe they were hairy people that lived secluded to escape ridicule. I wondered at times if they were aliens, "left-over" neanderthals, government experiments went wrong, or even some strange monkey living in the United States. One thing remained constant.

I always believed that whether they lived in today's time or not, there was something to this mystery. At some point, these Bigfoot did exist. One thing I never considered until I was an adult was that they could be on the east coast- they had to live among the giant redwoods in the Pacific Northwest. Boy, was I wrong.

I always dreamed of going to Northern California and seeing one of these gentle giants. When I finally saw one of these creatures, it was basically in my back yard, right in South Carolina. I saw the peace and pain in her eyes. It was as if she were begging me not to follow her, I did not follow. My next encounter wouldn't be so peaceful.

This time, it shook me to the core, and I will never be the same. Now, I enjoy searching for these elusive beings but know to keep my distance. I have seen the power these creatures hold, and I have seen their dangerous side. I have felt a primal fear because of these creatures. There is nothing like fearing for your child's safety because of a creature that you have held so much respect for so many years for.

I have learned so much about Bigfoot, nature, humans, and myself by researching these creatures. I have grown as a person and seen my instincts flare-up on multiple occasions and learned to trust them more. I have also learned that there are good and bad in everything. Most of all, I have learned to research for myself and trust my instincts above all- especially when it comes to my children.

Melissa's encounter

South Carolina. Undisclosed location.

It was hard to pick the experience that I thought our readers may enjoy. In the past three years, I have had quite a few. Now don't get experiences confused with sightings.

I have had only two, possibly three, sightings. But over a few years, I have had more than my fair share of experiences.

Our team, The Carolina Cryptid Crew, had gotten together for an expedition. This was a well-known hot spot, but it was on private land, so we had very little chance of running into anyone else in the woods.

I was feeling a little apprehensive that evening and wasn't quite sure why. I had been on this particular property before, so the terrain wasn't new to me. Yet I had butterflies in my stomach. I kept questioning why I felt this way, there just wasn't anyone thing I could put my finger on. I kept trying to ignore this feeling and enjoy our evening out with the team. I kept telling myself that once I got out into the woods, everything would be fine.

Our team grilled some hot dogs and had dinner together that evening. Which is actually pretty standard for us. We all get along great and enjoy each other's company.

We had cleaned up from our meal, and it was time to gear up and hit the woods. The feeling of doom and gloom was still hanging over my head like a dark cloud.

I had strapped my knife to my hip and hung my stun gun from my waist. I slid my digital recorder into my back pocket and slipped my camera onto a lanyard around my neck. I was standing at the table about to choose my walkie talkie when Cari walked up.

"Are you ready for this?" she asked.

"I'm not sure," I responded with a sigh. " I guess I'm just not feeling it tonight."

"Feeling a little nervous,"? She asked.

"I'm not sure what it is," I told her. " I just have this strange feeling in my stomach."

" I know," she said. " I have felt that all day myself."" Let's just stick together tonight".

I agreed with her and grabbed a walkie talkie from the table.

We split up into three teams, Team A consisted of Brandon and Chris. They headed to the right as we entered the woods. Both of them were familiar with the terrain.

Team B consisted of Marty, Michelle, Jean, and Laverne. Marty led them because he knew the woods.

Team C was Cari and me.

Cari and I followed team B out into the woods. We could see Team A's flashlights off to the right. From this distance, they looked like lightning bugs. As we went deeper into the woods, Cari and I branched off to the right as Team B stayed straight and continued on further.

Cari and I were familiar with these woods, and I was secretly testing a theory in branching off to the left. I had a gut feeling that they entered this particular stretch of woods from the far left. There was a fence line that led right down to the swamp. I thought maybe they used this fence line as a way to move up from the swamp and over into this stretch of woods.

Cari and I continued walking in a northwest direction until we found a big tree with minimal leaf litter. I took my foot and scraped away as much of the leaves and sticks as possible. I didn't want them crunching if we should move around a little. We turned off our lights and waited.

After a little while, Cari brought my attention to a small tree that was about a foot away from the big oak tree we stood under. This smaller tree looked to be about six feet tall. Upon closer inspection, we realized that this wasn't a small tree, but rather a large branch that had been shoved about three feet into the ground! We had seen these before, so it wasn't a big deal. I guess we just took it as another sign of activity. Now, looking back, I wonder if it hadn't meant something.

Cari and I stood there in the dark. The woods were utterly still tonight. No frogs or crickets made a sound. Usually, when the woods were this silent, we could look forward to some kind of activity.

My legs were beginning to grow tired of standing there. I wondered what time it was now. It had been around ten when we entered the woods. My guess was eleven-thirty or twelve.

I looked around the silent woods. Every once in awhile, I could see a faint glimmer of light coming from the far right. It was the area that team A was in. We began watching this light, and by the way, it would blink on and right back off as it was moving, it gave the appearance that Team A was following something. I knew they would never turn a light on unless they absolutely needed it. And moving was the only time it was required. As thick as these woods were, someone could get hurt without a light. And the tree canopy blocked out any moon that we may have had.

I thought I heard something in the distance, but I wasn't sure. I stood there, straining my ears to hear. Just as I heard it again, closer this time, Cari asked, "Did you hear that"?

I confirmed that I had. It was a branch breaking from the direction of the swamp, just down the fence line from us. This is what I had thought might happen. My theory was beginning to become fact.

I eased the walkie talkie out of my pocket and keyed the mike. I whispered, "We have some movement." The walkie talkie went dead and refused to come back on.

Great! I couldn't reach our team members, and I had just placed myself and my daughter in law in the very path that I had assumed these things used to gain access to this particular part of the woods. Maybe that hadn't been such a good idea. I was wishing now that one of the men had come with us. They carried guns, we didn't...yet.

We heard branches breaking again, even closer than they were last time. My heart rate was beginning to pick up. Now I could faintly hear footsteps. The leaf litter I had worried about earlier was now crunching under something else's feet. The steps were slow, to begin with, but as we listened, they gained speed and was closing the distance between us pretty quickly. Hearing these footsteps, there was no doubt in my mind that this was something bipedal.

I grabbed hold of Cari's arm. These footsteps had gone from a slow walk to a fast walk as we stood there in the dark listening. I knew whatever this was would be directly in front of us in just a few more seconds! My heart was racing now, and I was scared to death! The image in my mind was a Bigfoot approaching, and by the sound of its movements, it was pretty upset that we were there.

I knew that we needed to do something fast, but I wasn't sure what. I turned to Cari and quickly whispered, " follow me." 'We'll take three big steps toward these footsteps and turn our lights on. If it's any kind of animal, it's either going to freeze or run". This is at least what I was hoping would happen.

With my heart pounding out of my chest and my throat dry, we took those three steps and instantly lit up a big part of the woods. I was prepared to see a very tall hairy being standing in the beam of our lights. This thing could not have been more than four or five feet in front of us by the sound of the footsteps! But there was nothing there!

Before my mind had time to comprehend that we weren't faced with some bipedal monster, all hell broke loose behind us! Something large was crashing down through the branches!

Both of us immediately spun around to see a rock the size of a cinder block falling out of the tree we were just standing under! It hit the ground with a sickening thud.

We kept our lights trained on the trees for the next few seconds, but we couldn't see anything, and the night was just as silent as it had been.

Feeling very uneasy and knowing we were being watched, Cari and I decided to leave the woods. We both needed a break.

We weren't thinking clearly in light of what had just happened, and besides, we needed to grab a different walkie-talkie. We held onto each other as we slowly vacated the woods. The words, "walk, don't run" playing over and over in my head. We could hear movement in the brush to our right and our left. It felt like we were being toyed with. (A game of cat and mouse.) It seemed like we walked miles before we saw the lights of command central. We had been flanked the whole way.

I knew in my heart, I had a lot of things to think about that night. I wasn't even sure that I would be able to continue with the team...our team...the very group I helped to create. I may have to walk away from the things that I loved most. I would never be comfortable in the woods again. I can't honestly say, "a Bigfoot did this." But I know there is something out there, and it is Big.

Tye's Encounter

Des Moines river

It was around 10:30 pm on that march evening in 2015 when I had the most unforgettable experience of my life. As long as I live, I will never forget that night.

The evening air was crisp, and the stars were so abundant that I just had to walk 2 blocks to sit at the Des Moines river and stargaze. As I was sitting on the ledge admiring God's beautiful sky, I heard a rock get thrown in the river to my right. I estimated the stone to be about softball size according to the sound it made hitting the water. I really didn't think too much about it until I heard another rock hit the water. I glanced to my right briefly and turned my attention back to the stars. A moment later, there was the third rock, now I knew something wasn't right. As I looked again, I saw what I thought to be a man on his hands and knees kneeling in the reeds. Not twenty-five feet from me. I was startled to think, this guy is sneaking up on me to grab my legs. That is when I stood upon the ledge and took a few steps back. All I could make out at this point was the top of his head, he had dark wavy matted hair. Just then, it stood up. Instantly I knew this was not a man. My fight or flight kicked in, and I started to shake. It looked at me for a second and ducked back down to the ground.

The creature ducked and stood 3 times. The last time he stood up, I got a good look at him. He was covered in dark, long matted hair I could not see his face because it was also covered with the matted hair. We stared at each other for what seemed like forever, but in reality, only a few seconds. The size of it was overwhelming. The shoulder width looked to be about 3.5 feet wide.

My encounter was cut short as a car pulled into the boat ramp about 100 feet away, my natural reaction was to glance at the car, and I did. When I looked back at the creature, it was gone. I think now, why did I take my eyes off him? I still can't believe I looked away.

This encounter will forever be seared in my mind. The scariest yet most exciting experience I have had with the creature known as momo.

Cari's Encounter

South Carolina Undisclosed Location

As I mentioned in my introduction, I have had an interest in Bigfoot since I was about 9 years old. I always dreamed of seeing one but thought I would have to go to the Pacific Northwest to have that experience. I even wondered if they had actually become extinct. The day would come that I would see one of these mysterious beings face-to-face, right here in South Carolina. Basically, in my backyard. I would start to question everything I had experienced and known. While I got some answers, I ended up with even more questions than I started out with.

In June of 2013, the paranormal team I was a part of had our very first Bigfoot Expedition. We really didn't think anything would come of it but wanted to get the team members used to being in the woods and using the investigation techniques in an outside environment. You could almost call it a mock Bigfoot hunt. In the past, while walking in the woods, we had found a footprint and partial. Although we did wonder about Bigfoot, there was no certainty, and it was only a footprint. There was nothing else to go on, so we let it go- we really had no reason to think this expedition would yield any results.

On this particular night, we had also decided to do a live podcast, as I was the host of an up-and-coming paranormal podcast at the time.

The podcast would serve as an introduction for some of the team members, a discussion about what it means to be a paranormal investigator, and a discussion of the night's events and lessons. While Melissa and I were setting up for this podcast to go live, the other team members decided to go out and take a look around the woods. This was when things got interesting.

At this point, we have no idea what the guys are experiencing. All we are worried about is getting the computers, cameras, and microphones up and going, as well as figuring out the lighting situation. Melissa and I are sitting at "command central," making jokes while we are getting set up. We hear an acorn hit the top of a building and think nothing of it. A few minutes later, it happens again. Knowing that it is the wrong time of year for this, and the wind is not blowing, we look at each other. Just then, a rock flies from the direction of the woods and hits a charcoal bag next to Melissa, from when we grilled earlier in the day. Something is going on. We think someone may be playing a trick on us, so we decide to get a voice recorder and walkies and go take a look around that area of the woods. About the time we get to the edge of the woods, we hear a "whoop." It is textbook perfect!

We radioed the guys and asked if they heard it or if they made the sound. They did not make the sound, but one of them did hear it. When we finish talking on the radios, we hear a perfect tree knock. The best I have heard to this date. We slowly turn to look at each other. I start to radio the guys and, Melissa stops me, explaining that they wouldn't believe it anyway.

We go back to finish setting up for the podcast and start discussing what had happened. We considered someone playing a trick on us, but knowing that no one knew what we were doing. And that it was not widespread public knowledge at the time that Bigfoot makes tree knocks. After discussing the situation, we realized that it was not someone playing a trick- we had a legitimate experience. Finally, the guys come back so we can get started with the podcast, but they were too excited to get started right away. First, they had to tell us about what they found in the woods, an 18-inch footprint! This was about 10 o'clock at night, so we wrapped up our podcast and covered the print with a bucket and rock, intending to cast it the next day. Sometime during the night, the print was uncovered, and the rain washed the evidence away.

Over the next few months, we would hear yells and tree knocks occasionally.

One day in late July or August, we decided to take a walk and look for evidence and listen. I didn't know that my life would forever be changed by a walk in the woods.

As we walk along, Melissa is turning around to take pictures behind us periodically. You never know what could be watching you. As she turns around at one point, she notices that one small tree is shaking, and nothing else is. She alerts Marty and me, so we head towards this tree. Melissa stands back with the camera so that she can snap photos, and she has a high vantage point to lead Marty and me.

We head around the tree, but Melissa yells that she sees something move on the other side. This isn't just a tree, it is like a den of some kind. It is a tree with a lot of underbrush and even an opening. When she sees this movement, I double back so that we can circle the area and meet in the middle. When I get to the other side, I look up, and something is staring at me. It is about 7 ½ foot tall, with red hair covering its entire body, even its face. It almost looked like an Ewok, without the hood. We stared at each other for what seemed like an eternity, while I'm sure it was just a matter of seconds. When a creature like that looks into your eyes, it is like time stops.

I could see it from the chest up, but because it had so much hair, I couldn't see any gender details.

I did, however, feel like it was female. It may seem strange, but my instincts said that it was a young female that may have recently had a young one. Looking into its eyes, I felt like it was saying, "Don't follow me," I'm not sure if it was because of the sadness in its eyes or if they have some sort of telepathic abilities. As I said, I now have more questions than answers.

 The creature turned around, took a few steps, and was gone from view, but not from my mind. I still see those eyes staring at me. I turned around to go back up the hill and come face-to-face with Melissa, who has a look on her face that seemed to be in shock and awe at the same time. We walk out together without saying a word.

Once we get out of the woods, I look down and realize that I had a camera in my hand, as did Melissa. Even with cameras in hand, we were in too much shock to actually raise the camera and take a photo.

From that day on, my interest in Bigfoot became a way of life. It was no longer a photo in a book, it walked right out of those pages full of legendary creatures and into my life, and it was there to stay. Since that day, I have looked back on things that happened and realized that these beings were here all along watching us and only now are we watching them.

One of the things that I look back on quite often was the most terrifying thing that has ever happened to me. My husband and I were asleep in the bed when my little dog started barking outside. This bark was different- the dog sounded terrified, and I had never seen her scared before. I looked out the window and couldn't see anything, so I decided to go check on her.

Before I even got out of bed, I was shaking with fear. I tried without success to wake my husband. Since I couldn't wake him, I decided to brave the terror on my own and now wish I hadn't. By the time I reached the back door, I was so terrified, I was in tears. I got to my little dog and bent down to see if she was hurt or tangled. As I bent over her small fence, I heard the most horrible sound I have ever heard! Just feet behind me! It sounded like a woman having her arm ripped off right behind me! It was a high pitched, shrill scream! I made a beeline for the house, not even looking back. Something was out here with me, and I had no clue what it was. I even left my dog behind and made it to the back door as Melissa and Marty were coming out to see what that scream was. It woke them from a dead sleep. To this day, I can hear that scream. I have searched for the sound and no animal I have found audio of sounds like it. The closest I can describe is how one would imagine a banshee sounding.

I never thought Bigfoot at the time, but looking back, I wonder if I interrupted a creature trying to get dinner. It could have been after the dogs' food, after the dog, or even could have thought I was going to hurt her. I will never know for sure what happened that night. Still, in my heart, I believe I was standing no more than 3 feet away from one of these terrifying creatures, but I also know that if it wanted to do harm to me, it had its chance at that moment. I could not have outrun or outfought this thing.

Not too long after this incident, but still, before the thought of Bigfoot entered our minds, another strange occurrence happened. My husband and I were lying in bed one-night watching television. We were laughing at one of those adult cartoons when something very frightening happened. Something hit our back porch. The porch is partly connected to our bedroom wall on the outside of the house. All of a sudden, in the middle of a laughing fit, something hit that back porch so hard that it shook our bed! We didn't know what it was, but after talking about it, we thought we would find a big limb outside the next morning. We were wrong and could not figure out what was going on. Now, I'm sure it was a Bigfoot.

Since the night of our first Bigfoot expedition, it has been quite an adventure. There have been so many things happen that I'm not even sure I can remember all of it, but there are a few things that stick out in my mind more than the others.

One night, we had an expedition. After our initial walk-through, Melissa and I teamed up and found us a quiet spot in the woods. We found a big tree with a smaller tree beside it. Well, we thought it was a tree, but it was really a big stick driven into the ground. We thought this would be a good place, so we cleared the leaves around so that the leaves wouldn't rustle when we shifted. We stood there quietly for a while.

There was another group just over the hilltop from us. We knew that if we needed them, they were close by, as we were for them. The other team was much deeper into the woods. We all had walkies for safety purposes.

After a few minutes, we start hearing some sounds but weren't sure what they were. Then we hear very distinct footsteps coming from the direction of the fence line, but much closer to us than the fence. Melissa whispered to me that she was going to turn her flashlight on. She turned it on, and we took 2 steps and whirled around when we heard a crash behind us.

As we turned around, we saw a rock the size of a cinder block crashing down through the tree- as if something threw it while sitting high in the tree, we were standing beside. The rock landed where we had been standing. Of course, we zipped out of the woods as fast as we could.

Once Melissa and I got our bearings, we tried to radio the other teams, but the radio wouldn't work. We calmed down and decided to go see if we could find the rock that was thrown at us. We got back out into the woods and couldn't find the rock or the big stick that had been driven into the ground. We are standing there trying to figure out what was going on when all of a sudden, we are surround by footsteps.

It sounds like five or six huge bipedal creatures walking around us, but we can't see anything because it is so dark.

We just stayed close to each other and darted back out of the woods. We didn't go back to the woods again that night.

That same summer, my husband had a friend visit from Indiana. He is intrigued by Bigfoot, so they decided to take him for a walk through the woods one night to see if anything happened. While they went for their walk, Melissa and I decided to sit outside the woods and watch the treeline for activity. While sitting there, we notice something to the right of us towards one of the trails entering the woods. We get up and walk in that direction.

I stop as a see something large steps between two trees. Melissa keeps going because something else has her attention. I decided to start filming, just in case. As I'm filming, I hear Melissa say, "I see red eyes," and I head in her direction. I see them as they raise up and start heading in our direction. I'm standing there filming when Melissa says, "Let's go NOW!" and grabs my arm, pulling me with her.

We go inside to calm our nerves, although I'm still very curious. As soon as the door shuts behind us, we hear a bizarre sound, and all I can think of is a kid knocking a stick against a picket fence. I couldn't figure out what it was.

 That's when Melissa said, "It's like a gorilla beating its chest." That's precisely what it sounded like! My blood ran cold- we heard this from inside the house. We tried and tried to get the guys on the radios, but failed. Needless to say, we were nervous wrecks until they got inside.

These days, it is commonplace to see signs of Bigfoot around the property. We find prints more often than we ever thought we would, but with the ground being so hard, we don't see them as often as we would like. New tree structures are popping up every few months, and random new evidence found often. I never imagined that I would be able to have so many unusual- both frightening and awe-inspiring experiences in my life.

I want to end this with a word of warning. These creatures are not evil, but they are animals. They will protect themselves and their young at all costs, even if that means hurting you. While they are not all bad, just like other animals, some rogues may attack for no reason. More importantly, though, if you get too close to a young one or you seem threatening to them in any way, you may just face the wrath of a nine-foot or larger monster.

That doesn't mean not to go into the woods- especially if bears wouldn't stop you. Just be warned, and please do not go try to hug one. They are animals, after all. Even people are dangerous, just remember that, and you will be fine.

Karen H

Eastern Kentucky.

My encounter takes place on a cold April morning. It was Turkey season here in Kentucky, and nothing would do my husband, but for me to go with him. Now don't get me wrong, sometimes when his buddy Mike didn't go with him, I liked to tag along. I don't hunt, but I love the peacefulness of the woods, and the brisk mornings would leave me feeling invigorated. But not this morning, I just wasn't feeling like getting out in the cold. I actually halfway dreaded it. But nonetheless, I drag myself out of my warm bed and out into the freezing dark morning.

As we drove out to Nick's hunting spot, there were very few cars on the road. I guess people had felt like I had this morning and stayed in. I was wishing I had stayed home. This feeling wasn't normal for me. I loved being out in the woods with Nick.

I trudged along behind my husband, already feeling the cold through my warm clothes. I had purchased myself a fleece face mask a few weeks earlier and was feeling really thankful for it now.

Nick had a few blinds set up in the woods, I was hoping he would choose a close one today. I just didn't want to go all the way into the woods. I don't know why I felt this way, maybe I was coming down with something.

We walked past the first blind, and my heart fell. We were going in deeper. We soon came upon another blind, and Nick stopped. This blind was odd, I knew Nick had never built blinds this close together before. I stepped up beside him as he examined the blind. "Another hunter"? I asked.

He said that it would have to be a poacher because he and Mike were the only two allowed to hunt this property. Then he explained that this one seemed odd because someone had taken the time to carry branches here from other trees. This was a large oak tree, but it had white ash and poplar branches as well the oak, and not all of it was deadwood.

We found a few more of these strange blinds as we walked on to Nick's spot. Nearing the place, I could tell right away that something was wrong. All of the tree limbs used to build his blind against a large oak tree had been removed and piled up neatly next to the tree. Needless to say, Nick was pretty angry now because this left us no option but to trudge deeper into the woods, and the sun would soon be up.

We finally made it to the blind. It was large limbs propped up at the base of a huge tree. This was big enough for two people.

We climbed underneath the branches into a dugout spot. We both drew up our legs and leaned back against the tree, just as the eastern sky begins to brighten.

Within seconds of settling in, we heard the most horrible scream come from about twenty-five feet to our left. At this moment in time, I think my heart stopped beating.

I wanted to whisper and ask Nick what it was, but from years of hunting with him, I knew he was listening to see if this creature made another sound. This would give him a better idea of where it was and maybe even what it was.

This thing lets out another angry scream, and was noticeably closer! Nick sucked in his breath. He whispered quietly, "We need to get out of here, Karen, Calmly and slowly." He began to crawl out of the blind with me dead on his heels.

We got to our feet, and Nick grabbed my hand. We turned and began to walk the path we came in on. All of a sudden, there was a horrible sound of branches breaking. As if a locomotive was coming through the woods behind us! Nick began to walk faster, repeating," Don't run Karen" Don't run" Then the sound was beside us! Something large, walking hard, and breaking branches!

Nick's pace picked up to where I was at a slow run to keep up with him!

I was absolutely scared to death! I have never been so happy to see our pickup truck in the distance. Just as we broke from the woods, Nick yelled, "Run Karen"! We both ran as fast as we could for the truck. This thing lets out a horrible scream behind us, but we didn't look back. We jumped in the truck and got out of there!

I have since learned that there was probably a Bigfoot in the woods that morning. It had removed Nicks blind because it didn't want him there. And it had bluff charged us to scare us out of the woods. Mission accomplished! Nick doesn't hunt there anymore. And if he did, he would do it without me!

Heather Dodd

South East Texas.

My husband had rented us a cabin by the lake for the weekend. We drove up to the lake on a Friday afternoon. The weather was warm, and I was looking forward to getting some sun.

Brandon had been really excited about going. I kept asking him what was up, and all he would tell me is, "you'll see." So all I knew was that we were going to the cabin that he and his hunting buddy had rented last fall. I remembered this trip because Brandon's friend Chris had cut the trip short, and Brandon had lost all of the money he had paid for the cabin. The trip was supposed to be a week-long, but they ended up coming back in three days.

I grabbed my latest book from the bag at my feet and settled into my seat for a good read. We had a couple of hours drive, so this would give me time to do some reading while Brandon fussed at the other drivers.

He asked me what I was reading and then laughed when I showed him the Bigfoot on the cover. Brandon let me indulge my interest in Bigfoot, and didn't make fun of me. While he was still a little skeptical, I was a full-blown fanatic. I read everything I could get my hands on.

I watched and re-watched all of the documentaries. I even joined some groups on Facebook to read the stories from people that had actually seen them. I just couldn't get enough. I drug Brandon out into the woods many times, but I was yet to have an experience.

Brandon kept telling me he couldn't wait for me to see this cabin. It wasn't like him to get this excited about going away for the weekend. We had only been married for two years, and we didn't have any children yet, so going away for a weekend was pretty common for us.

He said I would love it because it was secluded and surrounded by woods, with a lake nearby. In my mind, he had just described ninety percent of rental cabins. I was just looking forward to laying on my float in the water with a beer in my hand and soaking up some sun.

I secretly hoped it had a nice kitchen and possibly a Jacuzzi. I had brought some steaks to cook one night along with a bottle of wine. A Jacuzzi would be the perfect ending to my plan. I stuck my nose back into my book, and before I knew it, we were driving down a long narrow road surrounded by thick pine trees. I could smell the water through my open window. The lake was close.

We passed a few cute cabins that were set back off the road. After a few more turns, we were on an even narrower dirt road. As I was beginning to wonder just how secluded this place was, we pulled up in front of a little cabin. I saw right away that it had a porch swing with pillows. I was already hooked.

If felt good to get out of the truck and stretch my legs. As I was trying to get some feeling back in my lower extremities, Brandon, with a big grin on his face, went to unlock the door.

I still couldn't understand why he was so excited about this place. We had stayed in cabins before.

I grabbed my bag from the front seat and followed him in.

He took me straight to the windows on the far side of the living room. There was a large back deck with a grill and picnic table. No Jacuzzi, but I could live with it. Then he told me why he had brought me here.

He said this was a prime Bigfoot territory. He then told me what had happened that made Chris cut their camping trip short. They had heard some howls at night. They had rocks thrown at the cabin and found all kinds of prints out back.

The last night. It shook the back deck and hit on the windows. Brandon said he had been fascinated, but Chris was terrified.

I couldn't believe he had done this for me! I was so excited! He knew I had been wanting to have an experience! This was like a dream come true for me. I wanted to pinch myself! I just couldn't wait for the night to come!

We did see a few prints out back in the sand. I had never seen an actual footprint on the ground! I had only seen them in books, online, and on TV. Naturally, I took tons of pictures.

That night we sat in the living room with the curtains open and waited. At about ten-thirty, we started hearing a few howls. I was so excited! The howls gradually grew closer. This had me feeling feel a little uneasy. But I was fascinated. When the first rock hit the backside of the cabin, my heart stopped beating! It scared me to death! I finally got up and eased over to the window. I saw it! Standing just out of the trees. It was huge! From what I could see, It had long choppy black hair. The skin on its face and hands was a leathery black.

I say black because it was dark. There was only a little light from the moon. We didn't have the back porch light on. We had left it off, so they wouldn't be scared to show up.

I saw this thing standing there! It was slowly moving back and forth while it stared at the cabin. I have never been so scared in my life! I was thinking that this thing could quickly get into the cabin and kill us! It was massive! Monsters really do exist!

This thing, let out a scream that shook the windows! It was loud! And it was way too close for comfort.

I had my experience, now I just wanted to leave! It was my turn to cut the trip short.

Brandon got some sleep on the couch while I sat up all night listening to the rocks hit the backside of the cabin. At the very first sign of daylight, I woke Brandon, and we headed home.

I still thank Brandon for my experience. But it was more than I was ready for!

Anonymous

Undisclosed location

As a teenager, I lived just outside of town. In fact, if I pushed it, I could walk to town for anything I needed- not that I actually did that. There were some sparse woods in my neighborhood, along with a little wildlife, including a neighborhood fox, beaver, and a black bunny that had escaped from my little brother's hutch. Although the homes have big yards, they are still reasonably close together. The people who live in the area range from young families, families with teenagers, recent empty nest parents, and elderly couples. Just as you suspected, it is the typical, All-American neighborhood.

My immediate neighbor on one side was an elderly lady who had never married or had children. I got close to her because she would hire me to help her out with housework and yard work. On the other side, it was my grandparents.

 Between the three homes, we enjoyed feeding the fox and watching out for the neighborhood wildlife. Life was normal.

My bedroom window faced the road, with the head of my bed beside it. My room was noisy from traffic, and it had a streetlight that came right in my window. I prefer to sleep in complete silence and darkness, but over time, I could sleep decently.

I was asleep one night, sleeping really well when my dog woke me, barking out the window. I looked where she was barking and saw this big hairy thing looking through my window. A bear was my first thought. Upon seeing this, I grabbed my dog, ran to the back bedroom where my mom was sleeping. Yelling for her on the way. When I got there, I handed her my dog and asked her to hold it. I grabbed the .22 from her nightstand drawer and went back. Mom's yelling and asking me what is going on, but I don't have time to explain.

I knew that a .22 probably wouldn't kill an animal of this size, but I wanted it just in case it tried to break the window. I thought that if I shot it out the door into the air, it could at least scare it away.

 Looking back, I probably should have grabbed dad's rifle, but I was young and not thinking. Also, we kept the pistol loaded, but not the rifle. I knew the .22 was ready to go.

When I got back to my room, the thing was gone. I went back to my mom's room to explain and process what happened. I'm telling her that it was a bear, without really thinking about it. I had assumed bear because there had been one reported in the area, and that's the only sizeable hairy animal around.

However, when I pictured the thing looking in my window, I realized that it was not a bear. This thing had hair longer than a bear does. It was standing with a hand- not a paw, pressed to the panes on each side of my window. Its head was even with the top of my window, but it was kind of leaning to look in. If you picture a person looking in a window, it would be similar. I could not see the details of its face because of the position of its hands. With the streetlight, I could see the length of hair and that its head was different- like a vast hairy person looking in my window. It took me quite a while to explain and process what happened that night, and I was stunned. I didn't want to admit it, but the only explanation I could come up with was that a Bigfoot was looking in my window. I must have lost my mind from the stress of high school because surely these things do not actually exist- do they? I did not sleep much that night, hoping that nothing like that would ever happen again.

I could have investigated further to get the answers to everyone's questions. Still, I didn't think my psyche could handle it.

I would not be able to sleep at night with confirmation that this thing was looking through my window. In my heart, I know that is what I saw that night, but I do not need physical evidence or investigators to confirm what happened that night. That would make it too real.

I try to not think about that night often, or the nightmares may come back. However, occasionally, the memories come back, and I question many things. I've thought maybe it was looking for food, but the kitchen was at the back of the house, and there is actually coverage from human eyes there. My window was out in the open and visible from the street. Why was this thing looking through my window- that is when I force the thoughts away. I've heard stories about Bigfoot since- some are quite scary, and I have often wondered what would have happened if my dog had not woke me.

Anonymous

Undisclosed Location

I was raised in the Air Force. I had the unique experience of living all over the world. I'd lived in or visited 48 states, including Hawaii, had visited 8 countries, and lived in Okinawa before I was 13. I had terrific experiences but had always wanted to live on a farm.

When I moved to a small town in South Carolina at the age of 16, and my dad had retired, it was a different world. I would end up getting married, having 3 kids, and searching for my farm.

In the mid-nineties, I was excited to finally find a family home out in the country. My husband and I had moved around a lot, and with children who were 10, 8, and 4, we were looking to finally find a permanent home. There was a small town we were interested in, that was still not too far from our families. We could get to them quickly if we were needed. With them aging, this was particularly important. The property we found was perfect.

This property was a few acres, surrounded by cow pastures, fields, and woods. The driveway was long, and the main road could not be seen from the property. There was an old farm-house that an elderly couple lived in just off the main road. They were our closest neighbors.

My kids could be as loud as they wanted, with no one complaining. This was the property we were going to rent, with the possibility of purchase after a year. It was my dream.

Along with a home large enough for all five of us, the property contained a storage building and a barn that would be perfect for chickens. A field for planting a garden. And there was a cherry tree in the center of the yard. On one side of the property was a cow pasture. The rest of the property was surrounded by dense woods. The entire long curvy driveway was lined with blackberries on both sides. This was my dream, and I knew we would have years of fun to come.

I was already planning gatherings and fun days with the kids. There was going to be plenty of time to prepare since spring was just about to start. We were going to get moved in and spend our days cleaning up the property, planting a garden, and getting ready for chickens. We were going to start there, and once we were in a routine, we would add different things in. Eventually, I wanted a milk cow, a couple of pigs, and maybe even horses for the kids to ride; but that would be years down the road.

Eventually, we did get settled into a routine. Soon, the kids would be out of school for the summer, and the fun would really begin.

My husband and I had a garbage pick up service. While he did the routes in the morning, I did the paperwork, and then we had the rest of the day to focus on family and our little farm. Life was perfect, but I was still living in bliss at this point.

About the same time, the kids got out for the summer, I started noticing strange things. The garden had never produced except for green onions. Things would bloom, and even produce vegetables, but when we went to pick, they would be gone. The cherry tree never had fruit on the bottom half, and the blackberries on one side were always picked. I thought it was strange but assumed that it could be just animals in the area.

The chickens were a different story, sometimes in the middle of the night, they would be making so much noise that it would wake the whole family. We wouldn't see anything when we looked out. However, the next morning, either all the eggs would be gone, or a chicken would be gone. I thought it strange when one morning, there were about 5 feathers lined up straight, but it could have been one of the kids.

My husband taught my daughter how to take care of snakes and weasels when they would get in with the chickens. Since she is the one taking care of them, he taught her how to empty an egg and fill it with salt.

That would keep them away. My husband had done this since he was a little boy, yet it didn't work here.

One day, the kids were playing outside when I heard a truck coming down the driveway. I assumed it was my husband coming in from work until my daughter was screaming for me that they had guns. I did not know what to think, so I grabbed my revolver on the way out the door. I couldn't believe what I saw. A group of about 7 farmers is seen standing in my yard, holding shotguns. I sent the kids to the house and took care of business. In some, not so nice words, I explained that they needed to get their sorry butts out of my yard with those guns. I didn't appreciate them showing up like this with my kids in the yard. They did apologize for scaring the kids but explained that they were going to shoot my dog. Oh, no, they were not! My dad gave me that dog since we were out in the middle of nowhere.

They went on to explain that cows in the area had been killed, and one of them saw a large black shaggy dog take down a cow and that ours was the only one like that in the area. Our 14-year-old black chow could not have possibly taken down a cow. Once I explained that he was that old and basically for show, they calmed down. When they saw the heavy chain he was on, they realized that our dog could not have possibly been the culprit.

They did apologize again and gave me their phone numbers in case we ever needed anything. I didn't want anything to do with them and told them that. They understood but insisted that I call if I ever needed them, even in the middle of the night. They seemed to know something I didn't, but I let it be.

Strange things like this would continue to happen, but this would remain my dream home for a while. There was something peaceful about sitting outside at night and listening to the sounds of the country. I would usually go inside about the time I would start hearing coyotes and other animals howling. Something was unnerving about the howls.

One particular night would change my life and my opinion of this place forever. The kids were still out of school and wanted to stay up late. I let them, and we watched movies until they finally drifted off. My daughter was my movie buddy, so she was awake a while after her brothers.

At about 10 o'clock, the dogs started barking pretty good, but I didn't see anything. A few minutes later, there was some noise out back, and pebbles began hitting the big picture window on the backside of the living room. My daughter started to look out, but I told her to stay put. I got up and looked out. There was a security light, so I got a decent look at what was out there.

I could not believe what I saw. A huge monster was standing in my back yard, staring back at me. This thing had to be at least 9 foot tall, was covered in shaggy hair, and had the most menacing eyes I have ever seen. I was terrified. All I could focus on was those eyes. A human I could fight off in the name of my children, but how in the world could I fight a monster? This thing looked as if it could just rip the door right off and walk-in where ever it saw fit. My daughter asked me what I saw, and I told her nothing, although she could see on my face that it was something. I rushed the kids off to bed and had a long night of thinking ahead of me.

I had seen this thing before, but it was in my daughter's books and on television. My daughter was a little obsessed with these things, but Bigfoot wasn't what she thought it was. It was a monster. I knew I couldn't tell her what I saw, or she would be in the woods looking for it. I also knew that my children would not be out of my sight on this property.

No more playing outside all day while I did my housewife duties. They would have to stay inside until I finished what I needed. I would even make them stay at the first few bushes when they picked blackberries. What was I going to do? My dream home turned into a prison. I would lie in bed and think of these things the rest of the night, and couldn't shake those eyes from my head.

The next morning, when my daughter got up, she noticed something strange on the window I had looked out. There were handprints, small, but bigger than hers all over that window. She asked why they were there because the back of the house was pretty high up, and the prints were on the outside. I dismissed it as raccoon, hoping she wouldn't realize that they have tiny hands and that there wasn't a tree close enough for them to have used. She let it go and made jokes about me seeing aliens the night before. Where her mind comes up with these things, I will never know. She and her dad had a good laugh, and we went on about our day.

When the changes started rolling out, the kids were upset but went with it. I allowed them to play their Atari while I cooked, so that appeased them. My daughter, on the other hand, wanted to read under the cherry tree and couldn't understand why she wasn't allowed to now but had before. She was upset but listened because she was a good kid.

 While life was changing for the kids and their summer became a lot less fun, I was making plans for moving us back into town. When it came time to move, no one was happy, but I was protecting my family above all else.

I have thought about that night many times since. And have wondered if the other strange things that happened could have been related to this monster.

It wasn't until a couple of years ago that I would finally tell my daughter what I saw. She had now become a Bigfoot researcher. She had joined a team of people that spent time looking for the elusive monster. I needed her to understand that I worried about her and why. So I had to confess what I had seen that night so many years ago. Her response is always- "would a bear keep you out of the woods?" Well, I do see where she is coming from, but I still worry. I have since heard that there is a legend of the Barnes Station Booger. This blew me away because we lived on Barnes Station Road. I guess other people have seen what I saw that night. I try to not see them as monsters, but rather as animals. However, anything in this world that I feel is a threat to my family is a monster.

Pam Stevens

Northern Kentucky.

As far as Bigfoot, UFO's, The Paranormal and things of this nature, my husband and I had no interest. It was never a part of our daily life. And to be quite frank with you, at times, we probably laughed privately at the people that did believe in these things. We sadly assumed them to be on drugs or delusional. Now, neither of us laugh anymore. And I spend a lot of my time trying to find out just what these creatures are and where they come from.

My husband and I have about five acres in rural Kentucky. Each year we grow a vast garden that produces massive amounts of vegetables. Both of us enjoy gardening, so we grow much more than we need. This excess produce is usually given away to friends and family, if not given away, it is sold at our local farmers market.

Two years ago, I started noticing that some of our vegetables were gradually going missing. It started out small, Like a whole head of cabbage, one watermelon, a couple of eggplants. Things that were too big for deer or small animals to be eating or carrying off.

We assumed that someone in the neighborhood was helping themselves. We didn't really mind. If someone needed it, then they were welcome to it. We would have given them some vegetables had we known who it was.

This went on for a couple of weeks. Random things were going missing. Then the whole baskets started going missing.

My husband and I would spend all day picking produce and washing it for the farmers market. Then it would be put into large wicker baskets to display for sale. We left these baskets in the back of Mark's truck overnight. Then they would be ready to go the next morning. It started out that a whole basket of cantaloupe disappeared! We found the basket about thirty feet from the truck with three melons left in it and two on the ground. This was going a bit far. No one can eat that much cantaloupe. There had to be at least twenty-five in that basket. Someone must be stealing from us and reselling it.

During the week, random vegetables would be missing. Then on Saturday morning, a whole basket would be missing from Mark's truck. We didn't mind the random items, but stealing full baskets had to stop, so Mark put up some trail cameras and motion lights.

The first night the motion lights went off was on a Friday night. Just as the light came on, there was a blood-curdling scream! It sounded like it came from an animal, but it was no animal either of us recognized.

Mark grabbed the gun and ran outside. There was nothing there now, but a full basket of eggplant dropped on the ground! When you have a whole basket of eggplant, it has some weight to it. I can't carry one by myself. We were both puzzled now. We picked up the vegetables and went back inside.

A Couple of weeks went by and the baskets weren't taken anymore. We assumed that the motion lights had scared off whoever it was.

The random things in the garden were getting gone, but not the full baskets. We were fine with this.

One day Mark and I were out working in the garden when he called me over to show me something. There was someone's bare footprint. We knew it wasn't either one of us because we both wore boots due to the snake possibility. I was contemplating neighbors sneaking into our garden when Mark showed me something. He put his size thirteen boot right up against this footprint. I was shocked to see that his foot looked small in comparison! This had to be a huge person! But that would explain why they were able to pick up the baskets.

As time went by, we started noticing the footprints were showing up each time the vegetables from the garden went missing. We weren't having any more trouble with the baskets from the truck. The motion lights stopped whoever that was.

A few weeks later, I had stayed home while Mark took the produce to the Farmers market. I was out working in the garden when Marks truck came down the driveway followed closely by another pickup truck that I didn't recognize.

Mark introduced this man to me and told me he was here to look at the footprints. It seemed Mark had mentioned it to someone at the farmers market, and this man had overheard them. He had introduced himself and asked if he could come out and see the prints.

He took some measurements, a ton of photos. Made some plaster casts. And then asked if he could look around the property. I thought he must be playing detective when Mark explained that this man was actually a Bigfoot researcher. There had been some sightings in this general area. I didn't know what to think of this at all. Especially when Mark assured me that he was being serious.

The man told us that this was a definite sign of Bigfoot, and he had seen tree structures as well. He said there wasn't much we could do about them stealing the vegetables, but if they got to be bothersome to give him a call. He gave us his card and asked if he could come over one night and observe the garden. We told him that he could.

A few nights later, he came over about dark. Mark asked him if we could sit out with him. He told us we could if we didn't speak at all, that he was simply there to observe. We agreed and walked down to the lower part of the yard with him.

After a few hours, we saw what looked to be a huge dark shadow come from the woods and walk up to the garden. It had the shape of a man, but much bigger.

 It walked around the garden, bending over a few times, then it stood up and looked around, almost like it could feel us watching it. Then it walked away the same way it had come.

Mark and I were both speechless. But the man said that was what he had expected. We asked why he didn't try to take pictures, and he assured us that it would be impossible. He shook hands with Mark, thanked us both and left.

That was the first Bigfoot Mark and I had ever seen. But now, many years later, we have seen a few more. But this time, it wasn't on our own property. It was while researching with our team. We have been avid Bigfoot researchers ever since that night in our garden.

Anonymous

Walhalla South Carolina

I have always loved to go camping. My family camped a lot when I was growing up, and it is something I continued to do as I became an adult, although my parents stopped once we were grown. One year for my birthday, my parents bought me my own camping gear. I no longer had to borrow theirs, and I could go whenever I wanted. They even had me set up for primitive camping if the mood struck. Whenever I would have a few days off work, I would load up the car, call some friends, go pick up supplies, and head out.

I had been camping with my new gear a few times at family campgrounds but was getting tired of the kids walking through the site, the noisy camp neighbors, and the cars driving by. I was wanting solitude and pure relaxation. I wasn't going to get this unless I go out in the actual wilderness, which was definitely fine by me. I started making plans and promised my parents that I would take friends and a gun, especially since the place I had my eye on was outside of cell service.

The time was here, and I was finally going to get my few days of peace. I had picked out the perfect spot right by the waterfall. My days off were during the workweek, so I was going to have the place to myself, aside from my buddies.

I loaded the car up and was going to head out after work that evening after picking up some groceries for the trip.

Looking back, I should have just gone home that night. I ended up getting off late that day, so that was going to put me setting up camp after dark, but I didn't care- I was ready for some relaxation. Everything was taking longer than usual, putting me further and further behind schedule.

I even had to go back into the store a couple of times after realizing I had forgotten things. About the time I got out of town, I realized that I should have let one of my friends drive their cars, as mine set pretty low, and it was going to scrub the ground. If someone got hurt, I wouldn't be able to get them back to town quickly. I should have waited until the next morning, but I trudged on.

After a long drive out of town, a few miles down a rough dirt road, and a great time with goofy friends, I finally arrived at my destination. We all pitched in and got the gear to camp. Some of us set up, while some started a fire for dinner, and even got started on hot dogs for everyone since that would be the quickest.

I was helping set up the tent and then moved on to getting camp organized so that we could spend the rest of the time relaxing. The whole time I had the strange sensation that someone was watching me, but kept shaking it off as it is because it was dark and we were all so busy.

Even the footsteps I was hearing could have been my friends walking around.

We all sat down to eat and goof off. It was pretty late by now, but we didn't care. We were young, carefree, and having fun. Soon enough, I had to use the lady's room. However, since this was primitive camping, I had to go find a bush. I grabbed my shovel and went off on my own. When I was just about finished, a werewolf jumped out from behind a tree and scared the daylights out of me. I hear a roar of laughter and soon discovered that my hilarious friends had brought Halloween masks. Being the tricksters they are, that was the perfect time to scare me!

After I caught my breath and slowed my heart, we all had a good laugh at my expense. We had plans of sitting around the fire and discussing life probably until the sun came up. Sitting around the fire, catching up, we were laughing and having a good time.

Soon enough, I start hearing footsteps in the leaves and assume that one of my awesome friends is up to more tricks. Then, I start feeling like I'm being watched and begin to feel uneasy. Without really realizing that I was doing it, I started moving my chair closer to my friends.

The footsteps continue, but now there is another set coming from the other side of the clearing. Now, I feel like I'm in a horror movie, and we are being flanked.

All of a sudden, something makes a noise in the river. It sounds like someone splashing around. I try to tell myself that it is my hilarious friends playing a trick. A rock hits one of the girls in the group, and she yells for one of the guys to stop throwing rocks. Another hit beside my foot. We look around, and the entire group is sitting around the fire. We are not missing a single person. Then, the rest of them start hearing the footsteps. We even heard a strange whistle that sounded similar to the person, but not quite right.

 One of the guys in the group, who is an avid hunter, says that the whistle is a bird, and the footsteps are probably a deer, but what is in the water? A fish flopping, of course.

Well, I'm not satisfied with these explanations and feel like there are people out there. I'm not sure if they have ill intentions or maybe they are just playing a joke. Either way, scenes from Deliverance pop into my head.

The fact that we are camping just a few miles from where it was filmed did not help either. I realize at this point that I forgot to put my gun in the car. A sense of panic rises, and I'm starting to really get scared.

Even though I'm feeling really uneasy, we continue our night and try to forget the strange occurrences. Because of these things happening, we decided against having a beer that night and to wait until the next night. So to answer any questions, none of us were intoxicated. I'm trying to focus on my friends, but my eyes keep wandering to the tree line. Then I see it. This colossal thing that stood like a man stepped out from behind a tree. It was too far away for me to see anything except the size and the shagginess of its hair. It was terrifying and much larger than any human I have ever seen. This thing was at least 9 feet tall. Just as quickly as it stepped out, it was gone again. I didn't have time to get anyone else to look. When I told them what happened, they insisted it was my imagination, but I could see the concern in their eyes. Everyone was terrified.

We decided quickly to call it a night, and instead of one of the guys sleeping by himself in a tent, I insisted the whole group sleep in my big tent. We were a little crowded, but everyone was together. We even discussed leaving, but with the long drive and the rough road, we thought it would be safer to stay the night. That could have very well been the wrong decision. Throughout the night, an uneasiness continually hovered in the tent. No one was sleeping, and the funny guys were trying to lighten the mood, but it wasn't helping.

Throughout the night, pebbles were hitting the tent. I could have sworn that I was hearing someone walk around the tent. The moonlight was even being blocked. Hearing the footsteps and snorting, it sounded like a giant out there. I just knew whatever was out there was about to rip the tent up. We were all as still as could be.

I know there is something out there, but my friends are insisting it's just a bear- but a bear would not be walking around like a man, and wouldn't be this large in the area we are in. A bear will snort like we are hearing, but it isn't as powerful as what we are hearing. This goes on for a while longer, but the walking is getting a little further away. The rocks start hitting the tent again, and some even hit the river behind us.

The most horrible thing I have ever heard came next. This scream- like something is being murdered rings out loud and clear. As soon as this happens, everything else stops. We do not discuss it, we all try to fall asleep. We dosed, restlessly through the night.

We woke the next morning, and I realized that we all huddled together. We all rushed to pack up, made sure the fire was out, skipped coffee, and started heading out. We haphazardly took camp down, cleaned up, threw everything in the car, and we were out of there.

None of us spoke a word while this is happening, but we cannot wait to leave. All the way back to town, we didn't talk. I guess we were each processing our thoughts, but there was no desire for conversation.

In fact, to this day, we have not talked about it openly. When it is brought up among ourselves, the conversation is cut short. This is the first time our story is being made public, but others should know that these things are out there.

I am not including names, my real name, or the actual location. I do not want someone to put it all together. Some of us would face public ridicule and could risk their jobs, and others would be the laughing stock of our small town. We have no answers, but there is only one explanation. We were among the giants of the forest. The legend of Bigfoot walked into our lives that night, and as much as we try to escape it, we cannot.

Angela Brady

Undisclosed Location

My encounter takes place in the late spring of 1983, I was Sixteen years old.

My cousin had come to spend spring break at our house, and she and I were bored. We came across my father's old camping equipment in the storage building. Now, this gave me some ideas!

Mom and Dad used to take me and my two brothers camping when we were young. We always had so much fun on these trips; it made me wonder why they stopped taking us.

We put the tent up in the backyard to make sure there were no holes in it. Amazingly, it didn't have any. Then we went through the rest of Dad's gear to see what else we could use.

We didn't know if mom and dad would even let us go camping, but the thought had us excited, and going through all of the old gear had given us something to do.

We found some sleeping bags and some old lanterns, along with a few rusty spears for roasting hot dogs. There was quite a bit of other stuff there too, but we knew we wouldn't need a whole lot.

When Dad got home from work, we asked him if we could go camping. He and mom were not at all thrilled with the thought of us two girls going by ourselves. Megan and I begged and pleaded with them until they gave in.

Mom called around to all of the local campgrounds, and it seemed they were all booked for spring break. We were about to give up when Dad remembered the State park. Luckily, they still had a few places open. They said these were for primitive camping and somewhat secluded, but that was just fine with us!

Dad got off work early the next day so he and mom could drive us out to the state park. There was only one campsite left when we got there, and it was all the way at the very end of the campground. This campsite faced the lake with a large row of thick trees blocking us in all other directions. It was very secluded.

Dad helped me put the tent up while mom and Megan carried our stuff down to our pic-inc table. Dad walked around the campsite, checking it out to make sure it was safe. Then he went over all of the safety precautions a few dozen times. I finally got him, and mom both assured that we were going to be just fine, and we had no intention of swimming or going anywhere alone. We promised to stick together.

After my parents finally left, Megan and I unpacked and got our camp set up. Once we had all the chores done, we changed into our bathing suits and went swimming. After such strenuous hot work, the water felt amazing! We didn't realize how long we had been playing in the water until I noticed how low the sun hung in the sky. We would need to get out and get a fire started before dark.

Getting the fire started would prove harder than we thought. We combed the edge of the woods, but most of the dead tree limbs had already been carried off by other campers. We slowly picked our way further into the woods. This was not an easy task being that we both were wearing flip flops, and we knew there could be snakes close by.

After four or five painstaking trips from the woods to our camp, we thought we would have enough for the night. But just to be safe, I was going to light both of the lanterns tonight.

After we had a roaring fire going and both lanterns lit, Megan and I changed into jean shorts and tank tops before roasting wieners for hot dogs.

After dinner, we sat by the fire and watched the moonshine across the lake. We talked about going fishing, but neither of us really wanted to deal with any fish tonight.

We just sat there with random bouts of talking and silence until we were both exhausted. I carried a bucket of water up from the lake and put the fire out before we went to sleep.

We were lying on our sleeping bags in the tent, waiting to fall asleep when we both heard footsteps outside. The footsteps sounded like they came from the woods where we had collected our firewood earlier, circled the tent, and then stopped in the front. A few moments later, we heard what sounded like rocks being thrown into the water. Whoever it was had walked on down to the lake. We assumed it to be other campers and fell asleep.

The next day was a blast. My brother and his girlfriend came by. We all spent the day playing in the water and lounging on floats. We got out to grab a drink or a snack, and it was right back into the water.

My parents showed up around dinner time with two large Pizzas and some sodas. We were all sunburned and tired, so the Pizza was amazingly good. I couldn't think my parents enough for bringing it.

My parents left right after the Pizza, but my brother stayed to help us gather wood and get a fire started. He lit both of the lanterns for me then checked to make sure we had enough food and drinks. I kept telling him that we were fine, but he had to make sure.

Once everyone had finally left, Megan and I relaxed in our lounge chairs by the fire. It wasn't long before we both fell asleep. The sun and swimming had worn us both out. I woke up sometime during the night. The fire was dead, but in the moonlight, I could see a really tall man throwing rocks into the lake. He would bend over and pick them up and then throw them. It looked like he was trying to find the most massive stones he could. I watched him for a few minutes. I decided to wake up Megan so we could go inside the tent. But I fell back asleep, not waking up until the sun was coming up the next morning.

Megan and I both were pretty sunburned from spending the whole day before in the lake. We decided to skip the swimming until evening and go for a hike today.

I had forgotten all about the man I had seen the night before. We hiked the trails for a few hours and then went back to our camp for lunch and a nap.

We waited until almost dark to gather our firewood. The bad sunburns were keeping us from wanting to do too much during the heat of the day. By the time we had carried all the wood we would need back to camp, the sun was setting. We were hot and sweating, so we hurried into our bathing suits and hit the water. It was amazingly cool on our skin. This was the best we had felt all day.

We swam and lounged on floats until late into the night, neither of us bothered to get out of the water and start a fire.

Megan and I were laying on floats watching the stars when I heard the first rock hit the water. With the direction we were facing, the sound came from behind us. I had forgotten all about the tall man until just now, and my heart skipped a beat. I slowly turned my float to see what made the noise. Just as I had feared, the man was now between us and our camp.

"Megan look," I whispered. She turned to see where I was pointing and sucked in her breath was a gasp. "Holy Crap"! She whispered excitedly. "It's a Bigfoot"!

I was thinking there was no way this was a Bigfoot. It just wasn't possible at all. She was just trying to scare me. There were no Bigfoot at our local state park. The whole time I was telling myself this, I was observing this thing. Its arms seemed too long to be a man, and it didn't stand quite right. But I wasn't close enough to see any detail.

We watched it throw rocks for a few minutes, then it bent down and scooped up what looked to be a fish. With the fish in hand, it turned and walked back toward the woods.

A few moments went by, and an excited Megan said: "come on"! She began to paddle her float toward shore. I caught up with her just as she hopped off and grabbed it up. She made it to the bank as fast as she could. She snatched her flashlight off of her towel and turned it on. There at the edge of the water, were some of the biggest footprints I had ever seen in my life!

We had no way to document the prints, and they had washed away before daylight. My parents picked us up that day. We both begged for one more night, but they wouldn't give in.

We went back and camped in the same spot a few more times that Summer, but we never saw our Bigfoot again. At times, I wonder if we ever really did.

Carol Sherman

Sawtooth Forrest

it was in August of 2007, and my grandson, Brandon, was here for the summer. He would be a senior when school started.Brandon lived with my son in California. We drove to the Sawtooth Forrest, about 28 miles south of my home. We had been at this location many times, even rode horses up there. We turned off at Maelstrom Hollow and went up the steep grade to get to the beaver dam.

I should have taken the first dirt road after getting to the top of the grade but passed it. When I realized it, I turned my truck around and went back to the right road. We had the windows down, it was a hot day, and I noticed it was very quiet, no birds singing, no noise and a very eerie feeling. Later, On the way home, Brandon said he had the same feeling.

About one mile in, I pulled off and parked we would walk the rest of the way to the beaver dam. I had my dog, and Brandon insisted on putting her on a leash. I said, OK, if you lead her.

The dam was about 1/4 mile walk from the truck.

We were almost to the dam when I stopped Brandon, an unknown fear had taken over me. I told him we can't go any farther or something terrible will happen.

The road had a slight curve, and I was looking at something tall and gray through the trees. I heard mumbling and smelled a strong odor. Brandon said he heard sticks banging. He froze, looking off to the west of where I looked and said, "grandma, there is something over there," then my dog barked with hackles raised. He said that whatever it was, it was hunched over and stood up staring at him, it had dark hair all over it. When it looked at him, he could tell it had bright yellow eyes. He was able to look away only when my dog barked. I said, "let's get out of here, but walk don't run." I said, "don't look like prey."

At that time, I didn't know what we had encountered. We were almost to the truck, I gave Brandon the key, and said, "now run and get into the truck." He said it followed us staying in the tree line. Brandon and Sheba (my dog) kept looking back at it. I was too scared to look. It was the evilest feeling I have ever had. Brandon said the same thing. We drove out, and that is when I finally felt safe again.

Anonymous

Delaware County, Iowa

I was about 18 or 19 years of age at the time, old enough to realize what I saw wasn't normal. All these years later, I still remember it as though it happened yesterday.

Sometime in the summer of 1959 or 1960, I was with my parents visiting my uncle and aunt on their farm in rural Delaware County, Iowa. Just at dark, we set off to visit my grandparents in nearby Delhi. Dad took a dusty gravel back road as a shortcut. As we were approaching an old bridge, something shot across the road in front of us. It ran on two legs, grabbed the metal pole at the end of the bridge to slow itself down, then swiveled and went sliding down to the creek on its butt. Mom said, "What in God's holy name was that?" I said, "I dunno. What was it?" Dad said, "I didn't see anything" (even though he had slammed on his brakes to prevent hitting it).

The image I've carried in my head all these years is that of a biped between 4-1/2' and 5' tall, covered with light brown/rust-colored hair. I can only guess at its height because it ran in a somewhat bent-over position as if to lessen its profile. Still, it was definitely smaller than an average adult human.

At the time of this incident, I had never heard of Bigfoot. It was several years after the Patterson-Gimlin film came out before I finally realized what we had seen. I'd been reading a book on Bigfoot, where the term "juvenile" was used. Sometime after that, the light bulb clicked on in my head, and I realized what we'd seen was a juvenile Sasquatch.

Whenever Mom and I got together after that incident, she'd say, "Remember the night that . . . ?" I'd say, "Yes," then we'd both say, "I wonder what that was!" I do wish that Mom and I had discussed it more, but we never seemed to be able to get beyond those few words. Dad would never talk about it.

My Dad was a hunter his entire life, from the time he was first able to shoot a slingshot. He prided himself on being able to instantly identify any animal/bird with just a fleeting glance. What he saw in the headlights of our car that night was something he could never wrap his mind around because he just couldn't find a category for it.

Now, I know what we saw.

Jackie Evans

Daggett County Utah

My husband Brad and his buddy Jason had planned to spend a Saturday on the river fishing. They would usually leave before the sun came up and not get home until late in the evening. My friend Anna (Jason's wife) and I didn't have anything to do that weekend, so we decided to tag along with them. We would do that from time to time on their hunting and fishing trips. The four of us always had a lot of fun together.

Before sunup, we were well on our way. We were miles out in the middle of nowhere, driving up some abandoned dirt road. This was supposed to be some great new fishing place. One of Brad's friends from work had told them about it. He also said for them to be cautious because bear and Bigfoot had been known to frequent this part of the river. We all knew to be careful of the bears when fishing anywhere on this river. But we all had a good hearty laugh at the Bigfoot part.

Brad slowed down and pulled the truck as far off the road as he could. Which wasn't very far at all with the thick trees lining the road. We got out and started gathering our gear from the back. The air was still a bit chilly since the sun hadn't come up, so I grabbed my jacket from the front seat.

The men had the gear while Anna and I were given flashlights. We would need them to find our way through the woods to the river.

Just as we started into the woods, I had a strange feeling of dread. I am not physic by any means. But I usually like to pay attention to my gut instincts. This time, however, there wasn't much I could do about it. I just told myself to pay attention and keep an eye out for bears.

As we walked, the group was talking and cutting up, but I kept hearing something in between our footsteps and everyone's chatter. After a while of hearing this odd noise, it was finally close enough that everyone else heard it too. "Whoop!" Everyone commented on the strange bird and speculated on what type it could be.

We continued our walk and arrived at the river just before the sun came up. I still had that strange feeling, but I was trying my best to push it to the back of my mind. I thought it might be best to go ahead and GPS our location just in case. I grabbed my phone from my back pocket and was not pleased to find no bars. We were completely out of cell phone range. After asking around, it was the same with everyone. No one had a signal. Brad joked about it doing us all good to be "untethered" for a while. This really didn't help my uneasy feeling.

As Brad and Jason got things set up to do some fishing. Anna and I walked a few feet upstream, looking around. I had to admit that this was a beautiful place. And I tried to let the sound of the river soothe my nerves.

Why in the world was I feeling this way? It didn't take long for Anna to pick up on my mood and ask if I were OK. I explained that I just had some stupid uneasy feeling. To my surprise, she told me that she was feeling the same way.

We decided that instead of fishing, we would pull our books out of our backpacks and do some reading. Maybe it would get our mind off of things and change our mood a bit.

We had been reading for about an hour when we heard that bird again. This time, it was just across the river from us. I kept looking in that direction, but I could never see it. From the sound of it, I only assumed that it would be pretty big.

After a while, the fish had stopped biting, so we moved on up the river. As we walked, I had that strange feeling of being watched. I was looking down, paying attention to where I was putting my feet when Brad stopped and grabbed my arm. I jerked my head up and saw exactly why he had come to a sudden stop. Not twenty feet away from us was what I can only describe as a Bigfoot.

Right in front of us was an enormous creature. It was kneeling down at the edge of the water. It appeared to be fishing. It would take its big hand and dip it into the water and then pull it back out. It would pick up a big rock, toss it into the water and dip its hand again.

We stood there watching this thing for what seemed like an eternity, but I'm sure it was only a couple of minutes. This thing had dark brown hair that looked thick and choppy. Its hands were black-skinned, and its head was almond-shaped. I didn't see any neck at all. I remember thinking that its arms looked too long for its body.

The bird let out another whoop from across the river. This thing stood up then and walked off into the woods. It didn't even look in our direction. Once I saw this thing stand to its full height. I was immediately terrified. It was huge!

Without speaking, we quickly made our way back down the river and then out to the truck. As far as we were concerned, this thing could have this part of the river all to itself!

I lost all desire to follow my husband hunting or fishing anymore.

Tara William Case

Brookings, Oregon

In 1991, I used to live in Brookings, Oregon, up the Chetco river about 7 miles. The land out there butted up against the Kalimiopsis wilderness. I worked the evening shift at a pizza place in town and had to drive the 7 miles home at around midnight. One night, I happened to notice something looking at me, "peeking" out from around a tree. I believed in Bigfoot at the time, and I immediately knew what I was looking at, but still found myself dumbfounded and in disbelief. I thought it to be a juvenile since it had more of a human formed neck and shoulders. I believed it to have not been matured, and it's muscles filled out along the neck and shoulders.

The next day, I mentioned it to my mother. She asked me where I saw it, and I told her. She had a shocked look on her face and told me that my dad had experienced the same thing around that area a few days before.

The second encounter took place around 1994. By then, I was married and had a two-year-old. My husband at the time and I went to visit his grandparents, who lived in a small town named Hyampom, California. It is located near Willow Creek. We used to hike out around the mountains that surrounded the little farmhouse.

There were multiple areas where gardens were planted, and about 200 yards from the house, there was a small vineyard where they grew grapes. Past that area, they did not maintain and let it grow wild. I noticed upon returning from a hike, as we approached the vineyard, there was a pile of dung. I knew by looking at it that it was not bear scat. It was an enormous amount and was very human-like in appearance. My ex did not believe in Bigfoot and convinced me to just drop the subject. Later that evening, I decided to take a bath. It was an old farmhouse that had the deep, claw-foot porcelain tub that took forever to fill up. There was a small window high up on the external wall that faced the small backyard. The way the tub sat, it faced the window. I saw a face looking in on me, and I just thought it was my ex playing a trick on me because I was taking a long bath. I proceeded to talk to him, saying things as I see him and that he wasn't funny. Eventually, he moved on. When I came out of the bathroom, everyone was sitting in the living room as if nothing was going on, so I let it be. The next morning, I wandered my way around the house and noticed the window was about 7-8 feet off the ground, and there was no chair or woodpile to stand on. I was taken aback, and realized what was looking in on me was not a man at all.

Maria Jansen

Undisclosed location

I, along with a few of my friends, were fresh out of high school and working at the local Dairy Queen. At night. After work. We had a favorite spot off in the woods where we would meet up with more friends and just hang out for a while.

My friends Sarah and Ron had clocked out at the same time I did. It was around midnight. We stood out in the parking lot a few minutes talking before we decided to go hang out for a while. Sarah had ridden to work with me, so we hopped into my car, and Ron followed us in his truck.

The place we hung out at was pretty far back in the woods on an old dirt road, but not quite far enough to be at the lake.

When we got there, there were already about ten others playing music and goofing off.

After about an hour, Sarah told me she needed to go to the woods for a potty break. It wasn't, but a few minutes later, we all heard her scream and came running out of the woods. She swore some big hairy man was in the woods watching her, and he had thrown a rock at her. One of the boys, being all macho, picked up a big rock and threw it in that direction.

Shortly after, the same rock came back out of the woods and landed in the clearing where we were all standing. Sarah and I, along with a few others, left right then.

A few weeks later, we heard that a fisherman had spotted a Bigfoot in the area. Some of the local kids claimed to have seen tracks, but I never did.

Sarah was my best friend, and I believe she saw what she said she did. I saw the rock fly back out of the woods with my own eyes. That was enough to keep us from going back.

Shelby Morrison

Lavonia Georgia

In June of 2015, our two sons (10 & 12) had just gotten out of school for the Summer. My husband and I always took them camping for a week at this time of year. It was just easier for us to go now, rather than wait until the campgrounds filled up.

The morning we arrived at the campsite, we were told there were only three spaces available, and those were primitive. (Could I do without running water and an electrical outlet for a whole week?) This is actually the way we preferred to camp. We just chose to go to the local campground due to the swimming access. Easy access to the lake meant that it was easier to watch the boys from the campsite while they played in the water.

We drove around and looked at the available sites. My husband, Alan, was not impressed with any of them. We talked about it for a few minutes. Alan decided to phone a buddy and get directions to a campsite on the river somewhere in South Carolina.

After a longer drive than I had expected or wanted. We arrived at the "campsite." Actually, it was a river we arrived at. There were no campsites. It looked like you were just supposed to pick a spot and put your tent up, so that's what Alan and I did. While the boys stomped around in the river.

In less than an hour, I had a chair in the shade and a good book on my lap. Alan and the boys were baiting some fishing rods. After spending some time lost in my book, my muscles had gotten stiff. I put my book down and stood up to stretch.

I looked toward the river but didn't see any of the guys. It was natural that they would move up or downstream as they fished.

I busied myself organizing the camp. By the time I was finished, the guys still hadn't got back, so I went inside the tent and lay down for a nap. I was sure they would be waking me soon enough with a stringer full of fish for me to cook for dinner. I stretched out on the air mattress and was soon sound asleep. I hadn't been asleep long when Alan woke me up.

They had not caught the first fish. He said someone kept throwing rocks in the water on both sides of them, and it was scaring away all the fish. If they moved up the river, The rock-throwers would move too. It was the same thing if they walked down the river. They eventually got fed up and came back to camp.

Alan helped me grill some chicken for dinner while the boys played at catching crayfish. With the squeals coming from the river, I think the crayfish were catching the boys.

Dinner was awesome. As I cleaned up, the guys went to find firewood. I heard their laughter and chatter off in the distance. I took a deep breath of the fresh mountain air. It was really peaceful here.

That night we all sat around the fire laughing and making S'mores. Something screamed off in the distance, we all speculated about what it could be.

Everyone was tired, so we put out the fire and climbed into our tent. Alan told us all a scary camping story about the man with a hook for a hand. We all laughed and went to sleep.

Sometime over in the early morning, Alan woke me up and whispered for me to listen. Something was grunting and snorting as it walked all around the outside of our tent. It was a bear! We weren't used to bears at our campsite, so I hadn't tied the food up! We lay there and listened as it kept circling our tent. My heart was beating so hard I could hear it in my ears! Was this thing going to tear through our tent and attack us? I knew Alan kept a pistol on him, but it was mostly to kill poisonous snakes. Not to take down a bear!

As we sat there on our bed, holding our breath, I saw what I can only explain as a huge hand push in the top of the tent! I let out a scream, a horrible scream! It woke the boys and scared them to death in the process. Alan got them settled down. Whatever it was had gone away now. I must have frightened it too.

Alan and I stayed awake until the sun come up, then We cautiously ventured outside the tent. There were huge footprints everywhere! We knew then that we had been visited by what is called a Bigfoot. We packed up our things that morning and left. We have no intention of ever going back. It will be the local campgrounds for us now.

Anonymous

undisclosed Location

I never in a million years thought I would be adding my story to a Bigfoot book, but thank you for the opportunity, ladies.

My partner and I got a call one night of a peeping tom out in the rural part of the county. The homeowner was apparently home alone and scared.

We arrived at the residence, not really expecting to find anything. Most perps are long gone before we ever come on the scene. Especially calls like this.

We approached the house while shining our lights around the yard. A middle-aged woman came to the door and invited us in. She said she had been watching TV when she saw this huge face in her dining room window. I noticed right away that this window was on the backside of her house. She said it scared her, so she let out an involuntary scream. Once she screamed, the perp kicked the side of her home. But then he moved around to the bathroom window and was looking in. She could hear him hitting the side of her house. She said it sounded like he was just punching the house all up and down the backside. It stopped just as we drove up.

My partner and I went out back to take a look. The homeowner showed us the kitchen door, turning on her porch light as we stepped out.

The first thing I noticed was how far off the ground this back porch was. We went down the steps and out into the back yard. This side of the house faced some woods and would be pitch black if the porch light wasn't on. I walked over to the kitchen window and looked up. There was no way any man could look into this window. It was at least nine feet up. When shining my light on the siding, I did see some places where it had been punched in. But this looked more like it was done with a baseball bat. These holes were just too big for a fist. My partner was looking up at the bathroom window, which was also about seven feet up. There was just no way a man was looking in these windows. But seeing the siding made it apparent that something happened. Just then, we heard this god awful scream come from the woods. We both drew our weapons and spun around to face the woods. The scream came a second time, then everything went silent. If I live to be a hundred, I will never forget that gut-wrenching scream.

My partner and I walked to the edge of the woods, shining our lights. Neither of us was going in those woods. We were both ready to leave. I think if the homeowner hadn't been watching us from her window, we would have probably left right then.

Luckily we didn't see anything, so we went back to the house. Just as we got back to the steps, my partner showed me a bare footprint in the dirt near the bottom step. It was massive. This thing had to be eighteen inches long!

We let the homeowner know about the siding and assured her that no one was out there now. We gave the usual dialog of, "call us if you hear anything else"e, and we headed for the car.

As we got into the car, my partner looks over at me and says, "You know what that was, don't you"?

Knowing what he was going to say, I responded with, " If you tell me that was a Bigfoot, I promise, you will walk back to town." He let out a long hard belly laugh, and that was the last we ever spoke of the incident.

Anonymous

South Carolina

The weather was getting warm, so my husband and I, along with some friends, decided to go camping. Now when my husband gets ready to go camping, he is not going to one of the local campsites. He is going way out in the boondocks to find his own spot on the lake or river, and that is exactly what we did. It seemed like we drove around for hours until we finally found this little dirt road. We turned onto it and drove another few miles until we came to a clearing. I could finally see the lake through the trees.

We were so far in that one of our friend's trucks wouldn't make it, so my husband had to go back up the dirt road and pick them up in the four-wheel drive. I had always wondered if being this far out was really necessary.

We unloaded the trucks, and all the guys crowded around the cooler with the beer in it. Yep, typical camping trip. The guys got all of the tents, canopies, showers and toilets assembled and put up. Then with their cooler of beer, they left to do some fishing. The ladies got the camp set up and organized, but not before we broke out our own bottle of wine. (We couldn't let the men have all the fun.)

Once the camp was set up, we grabbed some chairs and sat around talking until it got too hot. We changed into our swimsuits and walked down to the lake. We had all brought floats and inner tubes with us, but those would have to wait for later. We just wanted a quick swim to cool off.

We walked back up to camp and reclaimed or chairs in the shade. It wasn't long before the guys came back with a lot of fish for dinner. They had already cleaned them, so we put them in freezer bags and tossed them into the cooler until dinner. It was too hot to start a fire now. That would have to be after dark.

We blew up some of the floats, and all took a cooler down to the water until the sun began to set.

Our friend Jason was the one to bring up Bigfoot. He told us that this was a known hot spot for bigfoot activity. Naturally, he took some ribbing from some of the guys, but I was instantly fascinated. A few of us decided we would go have a look around after dinner tonight.

 The sun had set, and a gentle breeze had picked up. We were all sitting around talking after we ate when the subject of Bigfoot was brought up again. Jason told us that some of the best audio had been captured in this area, and there had been numerous sightings. He said that maybe if we walked out into the woods, we might see or hear something.

A few of us grabbed flashlights and headed off into the woods while one couple stayed at camp. We hadn't gone far when Jason stopped us and told us to listen, off in the distance we could hear something yell. I had never heard this before, so I can't say if it was a Bigfoot or not, but it was exciting. As we stood there listening, we heard something big walking around not far from us. This made me really uneasy. I didn't know what it was, and I really didn't want to come across anything out here. We walked a bit further and stopped to listen again. That is when we heard this god awful scream that sounded pretty close to us. That was it, we made our way back to camp after that. The couple that had stayed at the camp said they heard it too. We all speculated about what type of animal it could have been, but no one had an answer.

We stayed out by the campfire a little while longer, and then everyone turned in for the night. The night was so peaceful, all of the things in the woods were forgotten. The sound of the waves, frogs, and crickets lulled us to sleep.

The next morning, I was the first one up. I usually am because the minute my eyes open, I have to pee. I crawled out of the tent, thinking about heading to the edge of the woods. I saw our overturned table first. All of our snacks and paper cups from last night were now nothing more than trash on the ground.

Our cooler had been dumped out, and the garbage bag was strewn all around the camp. Two chairs had the legs broken off them, and our big fire log was about twenty feet away from the fire! Who would have done this?

Why would someone trash our camp?

Everyone was as shocked as I was. Why would someone do this? Naturally, all of us girls were ready to pack up and leave. The guys were hell-bent on staying Until we started seeing all of the big footprints all around the camp. The women were packing up; the guys could stay if they wanted too. We all left together. I don't know for a fact that we experience Bigfoot activity. But I do know I was ready to go and I won't camp there anymore.

Leigh K

South Carolina

I know that many people in my tiny corner of South Carolina only recently began to think there was a possibility of a Bigfoot being anywhere but the Pacific Northwest. Now, they only think it is possible thanks to popular television shows coming to the area. It was entirely out of the realm of possibilities for them to be in the upstate of South Carolina, well to most people. I'm not most people.

I've known since I was a young girl that these creatures exist and that they were literally in my back yard. The night of the incident, I didn't know what I saw, other than that it was a monster. It wasn't until a few years later, and I saw a picture of a Bigfoot in a tabloid at the grocery store that I knew what to call this beast. Don't get me wrong, it did nothing to me, except give me the feeling of pure fear when I saw it.

I was about eight years old. My Mom knew that I enjoyed scary movies and allowed me to if she deemed them age-appropriate. On this particular night, mom had promised me a movie night after my little brothers went to bed. It was a reward for good grades.

We watched one of those ghost movies of the eighties, something like Jack Nicholson would be in. After the movie was over, mom said it was time to bed and I went to snuggle in.

I'm not sure what month it was, but it was cold because I had to put an extra blanket on my bed, as it was next to the window.

Sometime during the night, I had a bad dream. Something had my foot and was dragging me. I woke screaming, and my parents rushed in. They got me calmed and explained that I had gotten my foot caught in my curtains. As I am sitting up in the bed talking to my parents, I looked out the window. I really wish I had not done that.

When I looked out the window, my breath caught in my throat as I saw a monster walk out of the woods behind my house and across the yard. My parents got my attention, and I looked away. When I looked back, it was gone. They asked me what I had seen. I tried my best to explain, but couldn't. It walked like a man, but it wasn't a man. They thought I "saw" a ghost and told me it was my imagination because of the bad dream. This wasn't it. What I saw was flesh and blood. It was a monster. It was very tall and solid black-darker than night. Although it walked like a man, something wasn't right. Its shape was off somehow.

I knew this creature was something real- something that could reach out and touch you. I also knew that it was not human.

I'm not sure how I knew, maybe it was just the fear I felt. I thought about it all night and had a hard time falling back to sleep.

The next morning, I begged my mom to help me move my bed. I didn't want to see this thing again. After seeing my fear and how serious I was, we spent the day moving my furniture around. Every time I looked out that window, I would think about it. I didn't even want to go outside when we had bonfires behind the house anymore. I stayed shaken up until we moved from that house.

A few years later, I was standing in line at the grocery store with my mom. I was getting pretty bored and had a bad habit of reading the tabloids. My mom always warned me about doing this, saying that 10 was too young to understand "that junk." I did it anyway. I couldn't help it, I found them intriguing. I look from one tabloid to the next for something that would grab my interest. It did not take long until I saw something and brought that night to the front of my memories. I grab my mom's arm and tell her that the picture had the thing I saw that night in it.

She was confused at first, but then realized what I was talking about. She dismissed me as letting my imagination run away with me, but I didn't have much of an imagination, so I'm not sure why she thought that.

I let it go but knew in my heart that I saw one of those that night. It had the right shape to it. Whatever it was that was off with the creature I saw matched up with this one. I read off and on about these creatures after that but didn't tell anyone else. They would have never believed me- they didn't exist in South Carolina, so they thought.

Jennifer Hudson

Lamar County Texas

I was born and raised in a little town in Lamar county Texas.

While I was growing up, I had heard of Bigfoot. It wasn't something I spent much time thinking about, but I would watch the documentaries with my two brothers. I guess I didn't actually consider it real. I had never seen one and didn't know anyone who had. So for me, It wasn't real.

It was Summertime, and my brothers and I were out of school. Just as we did every year, we were spending as much time as we could at the lake. We had a trail behind our house that went straight through the woods to the local lake. This trail was about a mile long, but when you're a kid, it doesn't matter how far you have to walk as long as you got to go swimming with your friends.

My brothers and I were both excellent swimmers, so mom didn't worry about us too much. Occasionally she would drive over to the lake and check on us. But most of the time, we were on our own. We would get there after our chores were done and stay until just about dark.

Sometimes she would let my brother pitch a tent with their friends and spend the night at the lake. I was never allowed to do this because I was a girl, But that was OK with me. Mom and Dad would pitch a tent in the back yard for my friends and me.

It was on a Friday, and my brothers were setting up their tent. We had been swimming most of the day when my mom came by with a late lunch for us. She had picked up burgers from a local fast-food restaurant. I didn't really want anything, so I had my soda while the boys devoured their burgers. After we ate, it was right back in the water. Mom yelled after me to start home before dark. I had walked home plenty of times without my brothers, so tonight wouldn't be any different.

The sun was starting to sink low in the sky. And most of my friends had already left for the day. I knew I should be heading home too, but I chose to stay just a few more minutes and help my brothers gather firewood. I grabbed the bag that contained my uneaten cheeseburger and headed for the path in the woods.

As I walked, I began to feel more and more uneasy. I kept telling myself that there was no reason to feel this way. I had walked through here many times, and a lot of them were alone after dark.

I had gone about a quarter of the way when I heard a snort that I wasn't familiar with. I stopped to listen. I knew that wasn't a deer. I stood there silently, but the woods were quiet. Actually, they were a bit too quiet. Usually, there was the sound of frogs and crickets with it being this close to the water, but tonight they didn't make a sound. I started to walk again, but this time a little faster. I kept scolding myself for being afraid.

This time, as I walked, I heard a deep grunt. It stopped me dead in my tracks. There was something in the woods with me! I had no clue what was out here with me, but I knew it wasn't normal. I kept hearing my mom's words, 'Get home before it gets dark" Now I was really wishing I had listened.

As I began to walk, I thought I could hear footsteps. The steps seemed to be matched up with my own. I needed to stop and listen but to stop walking was the last thing I wanted to do. I finally took a deep breath and stopped. I heard them! Three more steps right after mine! I was sure of it! Someone was in the woods with me! Maybe a serial killer? Some weird guy with an ax? Had they been watching us at the lake today? I was absolutely terrified. It was all I could do to keep myself from breaking into a full run!

For a split second, I thought about going back, but I was now about halfway, so it would be best to just keep heading home. Then I wondered if anyone would hear me if I screamed. I heard a low grunt and started walking again. I needed to get closer to home! If I got closer to the house, they might hear me if I started screaming. I pictured mom in the kitchen cooking dinner with her radio tuned to a country station and her singing along. Dad would be in the living room with the news on. The central air would be whirring along, and Baxter would be asleep on the back of the couch.

They would not hear me, no matter how loudly I screamed.

I continued my fast walk with my heart beating in my ears. My sweaty hand clutched the bag tightly that contained my uneaten lunch. I had forgotten all about it until I felt the cramp in my fingers.

The footsteps had begun again just as I started to walk. They didn't sound exactly the same as they had before. I was straining my ears, trying to find out why they sounded so differently. When I realized what it was, my heart froze with complete terror! These footsteps were now behind me on the trail! I stopped and spun around before thinking. There behind me was something nightmares are made of!

About fifteen feet away from me, this creature had stopped too. It stood there in the middle of the dark trail looking at me. I couldn't make out much detail because it was dark, so I am assuming the hair was black. It seemed to be about eight feet tall and about four feet from shoulder to shoulder. Out of reflex, I let out an involuntary scream that instantly made the back of my throat raw. When I screamed, this thing tilted its head to the side, much like a dog will do when it hears something it doesn't understand.

I began to slowly back away from it. After just a few steps, it let out a grunt that sounded like a huge monkey. It was a deep, throaty sound. It took a step toward me, and I let out another scream then threw the bag at it. I turned and ran for home as hard as I could run. I didn't slow down until I reach the back porch!

When I went inside, it was pretty much like I had described. There is no way they would have ever heard me screaming!

I went to my bedroom and sat down on the bed. My mind was still trying to sort out what had just happened. What had I seen? Just thinking about it again gave me the creeps. I would never be able to walk those woods in the dark again. I may not be able to walk them in daylight.

Where had this thing come from? Has it always lived here? I had so many questions!

I wanted to talk to my brothers about it but I knew they would never believe me and would tease me relentlessly. I fell asleep that night, thinking about the way it had tilted its head when I screamed.

The next morning I waited around the house until my mom drove into town, and I got her to drop me off at the lake. My brothers were getting ready to go swimming. They both asked what had happened to me last night. I didn't know why they were asking me this, and I was curious as to how much they knew, so I responded, "nothing," Why?

Then they proceeded to tell me that one of them got hit with my fast food bag last night while sitting by the fire. Naturally, they assumed it was me teasing them. And the other one kept hearing me scream really late Last night. How could they have heard me scream late at night when I made it home pretty early. I knew I couldn't tell them what happened, but I really wanted to. They said their friends told them that the screams were coming from a Bigfoot. A few of them got scared and went home. I laughed right along with my brothers. How silly to think there was a Bigfoot in these woods!

Laura B.

Undisclosed Location.

My husband "Greg" and I had just purchased a new home with about twenty acres of land. Most of the property behind our house was undeveloped. But that was fine with us. It was ours, and we could clear it whenever we found the need to.

Greg worked with the local electric company, and I was between jobs. I had been a hospice nurse, but my last client had passed away, so I was enjoying my time at home.

The first night in our new Home, our Pit Bull Sadie seemed restless. We were watching TV, and she would pace from the living room to the front door and whine. Greg had called her up on the couch with him a few times. Usually, she would lay down with him and fall asleep. But not tonight. We just assumed that it was the new house. She would settle down once she got used to it.

That night we were all sleeping soundly. Sadie was at the foot of the bed. She would whimper from time to time, but it wasn't enough to keep us awake. All of a sudden, she began a loud, urgent barking.

The sudden loud noise scared Greg and me to death!

Before we could even react to her barking, something, hit the front door! It felt like the whole house shook! My first thought was that someone was trying to kick our front door in!

Sadie jumped from the bed and went running to the living room! Greg got up and grabbed the gun from the nightstand. I didn't know what to do. I was terrified!

I followed Greg into the living room, where Sadie was still barking and growling. She had her front feet up on the door as if she wanted to get out there and take care of whoever it was. Greg eased over to the window by the door and looked out. He told Sadie to quieten down. He looked at me, saying, "There's no one out there."

"Then what in the world hit the door"? I asked him.

He said he had no clue, but he was going outside to check it out. I immediately grabbed Sadie's leash and clipped it on her. Greg and I both knew that once he opened that door, she would be out like a shot.

Greg went outside and looked around. There was nothing out of place and no sign of anyone having been there. I stood on the front porch with Sadie while she pulled, cried, and whimpered toward the woods.

We had to practically drag her back into the house! Greg slept on the couch that night while Sadie and I took the love seat.

The next morning we had three dead squirrels lined up by the front porch. Greg said he didn't know of any animal that would do this. He took them away and threw them out into the woods. Seeing the way they were lined up concerned me. This looked as if it were done by a human. But who and why?

The next few nights were uneventful, and it seemed as if Sadie was finally adjusting to our new home. She was acting more like her usual calm self until one night after dinner. I went to take the trash out to the back porch, expecting her to walk with me as she usually did. But this time, she tucked her tail and stayed in the kitchen. I teased her about being afraid of the dark and went on out with the bag of garbage. I put the trash in the can and turned to go back in when I heard something I had never heard before. It was a distant yell, but it didn't sound like any animal I had ever heard. I stood there and listened to this yell a few more times, then I went to get Greg.

Greg and I stood on the porch listening to this distant yell gradually get closer to our woods. Neither of us could pinpoint what type of animal it was.

The next day I took Sadie out for a walk. We went down to the woods at the backside of the house. The underbrush was pretty grown up here, so she was having a blast sniffing out the rabbits. She actually ran a few out and would have given chase if I hadn't had her harnessed.

I was just about to pull her out of the bushes and head for the house when I saw something in the dirt. It was a bare human footprint, and it was huge. I squatted down to look at it closer. Sadie came over to see what I was doing. She sniffed the print and immediately tucked her tail and tried to drag me up the hill to the house! The way the print was positioned was odd to me. This person was headed into the woods and not out. Who in their right mind would walk through there barefoot? You could see from here that it was full of saw briars and not to mention the snakes that had to be out there. I finally gave up struggling with her and allowed Sadie to pull me home.

Greg came home all excited that night and couldn't wait to talk to me. He said a man at work had told him that before we moved in that he had used this property for Bigfoot hunting. I didn't know how I felt about this. I was scared, intrigued, curious, all of these emotions flooded through me as I thought about the print I saw today.

He told me that the man would still like to bring his team over from time to time and walk through our woods. I told him that was fine with me, but I needed to show him something first. I took him down to the bottom of the yard, where I had found the print earlier. Sadie chose to stay on the front porch this time.

Greg was as shocked as I had been. We looked around but never could see the second print. We went back up and sat on the porch. We had a long discussion that night. Now everything was starting to fall into place for us. This is what had been going on with Sadie. This explained something was hitting the house, and it solved the three squirrels. If anyone had told me that I would be sitting on my porch discussing Bigfoot with my husband, I would have laughed at them. But this seemed to now be a part of my reality. Greg and I agreed that we would let the team come out as often as they wanted to as long as no guns were involved. We didn't want them harmed. If they lived here, it was fine with us. They hadn't hurt us, and we weren't going to allow them to be hurt.

Later on, Greg and I ended up joining this Bigfoot group, and we love being a part of it. For the past five years, we have learned a lot about this elusive creature. We actually enjoy hearing the tree knocks and the yells now.

We know that they are here, and that's fine with us. Sadie has even gotten used to them. Nothing about them upsets her anymore.

I think that becoming a part of this Bigfoot team has led me to understand them better and to not fear them near as much. I have respect for them now, just like any other Apex predator. And I feel very fortunate to be able to share my land with such a majestic creature.

Jenna Deveraux

Red River Louisiana

The subject of Bigfoot was as far from my mind as it could possibly be. I was a working mother with two young sons, a husband, two dogs, and a cat. I didn't have the time to dwell on make-believe monsters. So when my best friend Becky called me and wanted to go camping, that is not something that came to mind, like it would for some people.

Becky had been going through a lot lately. She had just lost her mother, and she and her husband weren't getting along, so her need to get away really didn't come as a surprise to me. I didn't want to go, but I didn't want her to go by herself. I told her I would be happy to go with her. I was already dreading it.

It was the fall of the year, but the weather was still warm. All of the public campgrounds were already closed. Becky said she knew a good spot that was just a short drive away. I took Thursday and Friday off of work and packed my things for camping. I kept asking myself why in the world, I had agreed to this. I knew Becky needed me, but a hotel room would have worked as well.

Becky's idea of a short drive was not the same as mine. We had already been on the road over an hour, and we had not reached our camping spot.

Finally, after an hour and a half, we turned off the main road onto a narrow dirt road that led into the woods. Now we were in for more riding, but this time, it was extremely bumpy.

I asked her how in the world she had ever found this place. She said her father used to bring the family out here camping because he thought camping should be free and was not about to spend money on a campsite. She said that she and Lee had been up here a few times, but it had been a couple of years ago.

We drove into a large clearing surrounded by woods on three sides with the fourth side facing the lake. It was absolutely beautiful. The ground sloped down to a small sandy beach at the edge of the water. Maybe this camping trip wouldn't be so bad after all. I could just see myself lying on that beach with a good book.

It didn't take us long to get the camp set up and then we were off to hunt for firewood. After half a dozen trips back and forth, we had enough wood for at least two nights.

We roasted wieners over the fire and had a simple hot dog. We watched the sunset over the water as we ate. The whole sky had turned a fiery red. It was simply beautiful. We sat and talked until late in the evening. Our fire was beginning to die out, so we decided to call it a night and get some sleep. We were both tired from the long drive.

We had both brought air mattresses for our beds. Drifting off to the sound of the waves breaking on the shore had not been a problem. I had slept all night soundly and woke up feeling pretty good. I had the coffee and eggs done by the time Becky came out of the tent. The morning was just as beautiful as the night had been. There was a thick fog over the lake, creating a magical appearance.

After breakfast, we took our second cup of coffee and walked down to the lake. Becky finally opened up about some of the things she was going through. We had a long talk, and she seemed to be feeling better about some of her decisions.

We swam and sunned most of the day. By the time we were ready to start a fire, we both were sporting mild sunburns.

That night after dinner, we decided to enjoy a pot of coffee while sitting around the fire, chatting.

It was well after midnight when we heard something moving around in the woods just past Becky's truck. We assumed it was a deer and didn't give it another thought.

That night as we lay in the tent waiting to fall asleep, we heard what sounded like rocks hitting the water. We thought that maybe the waves were crashing the stones just right to cause the sound. It wasn't bothersome, so neither of us got up to go look.

The next morning Becky woke me up telling me to "come look." She had gotten up before me and was going to make breakfast, but all of our eggs were gone! The cooler had been opened, and everything in it had been moved around. All of the eggs were gone, but the sandwich meats and sausages had been left. A large pack of hamburger meat was missing as well. Had someone come into our camp during the night and raided our food? Could an animal get the lid off of the cooler?

After finding the eggs missing, we decided to check the rest of the food. Our jar of peanut butter and a whole pack of Oreo cookies was also missing. We played it off as a Raccoon or some other type of wildlife. You learn to expect this kind of thing when you camp out. As long as we had our morning coffee, we were happy.

After coffee, Becky and I decided to walk around the lake and do some exploring. We were both still a little sunburned, so we would be swimming later this evening when the sun wasn't so intense.

We walked around the lake, collecting large pieces of driftwood. These could be used either in the yard or the house for decoration. About halfway, we heard a yell as we had never heard before. It sounded like it was just inside the tree line. We stopped to listen. After not hearing anything else, we continued on.

We hadn't realized just how far we had come until we started back. It was already well past lunchtime. As we neared the camp, I noticed that something didn't look right. Becky stopped in her tracks. "Oh my God, Jenna," she exclaimed.

 With a few more steps, I Could finally see what she was looking at. Our tent was down, and it looked like the whole place been trashed! Who would do such a mean thing!

We picked up around camp. The tent was ruined with three of the metal poles broken. We wouldn't be staying in that tonight! We were thinking now this had to be more a person rather than an animal. Animals don't break tent poles. But nonetheless, ours were broken now and useless.

We pulled our mattresses from the tent and threw them in the back of the truck. This would work for tonight. I only hoped it didn't rain.

We spent the rest of the afternoon swimming and sunning. We were trying to be positive and not think about what had happened. I had to admit this had been a relaxing few days, but I was ready to get home to my guys now. I was really starting to miss my family.

That evening we packed most of our gear into the truck. We would be leaving early in the morning. We couldn't stay without a tent.

Becky and I stretched out on a mattress and looked up at the stars. The sky was absolutely beautiful. I fell asleep watching the stars. Over in the night, I woke to the sound of Becky mumbling "stop it" in her sleep. I opened my eyes and looked over at her.

To start with, it looked like a really tall man standing beside the truck on Becky's side! My heart gave a leap! Then I realized this was too tall to be a man! This was a monster reaching over Becky to get to our food! I screamed at the top of my lungs! I have never been so scared! Becky sat up and while scooting backward began screaming too! This "thing" ran around the foot of the truck and off into the woods!

Becky and I scrambled to get into the truck! We drove off without looking back!

I know that had been a Bigfoot raiding our camp that weekend. I don't think that it intended to harm us. But it sure did scare us to death! Becky nor I either one has gone camping since that weekend, and I have no plans to.

Shannon Carter

Manasses Virginia

It took me a few weeks before I could get the nerve to write this. I want to thank Melissa for being so patient and understanding. Allowing and encouraging me to tell my story has been more helpful than you will ever imagine. (I changed names to protect my family. The location is real.)

My husband and I have always been fascinated with cryptids. Bigfoot being our favorite. We enjoyed reading books and watching TV shows. Like most people of our generation, we assumed these creatures to be in the North West with no possibility of them being local.

We had just moved next door to my husband's parent's in the spring of twenty fifteen. Their health was declining, so we moved closer to where we could help out.

His father owned roughly one hundred and thirty acres, and we were thrilled to be on the family property. Our twelve-year-old son was happy to have woods and a creek to play in while our daughter was delighted to have somewhere the dogs could run and play.

The area around the house had been cleared, roughly two acres each in the front and back yards. The rest of our property was past the back yard and uncleared. The trees were thick here with dense underbrush. Our son Matt was eager to cut a trail to the creek.

Phil's parent's home was about one hundred yards away from us. It was close enough for us to help out, but far enough away to give us all some privacy.

We were busy carrying boxes into the house when Phil's dad drove the golf cart over to invite us to dinner. Knowing that my kitchen was still packed up, we gladly accepted.

We enjoyed a wonderful dinner of hamburgers and hotdogs in the backyard. The weather was perfect for a cookout. After dinner, the kids ran to catch lightning bugs while we sat and talked. Phil's Dad, Nathen, got up to scrape the plates. I watched as he scraped each dish into a small bucket, once he was finished, he asked Phil if he wanted to walk with him.

I watched them walk to an outbuilding and go inside for a moment, then they continued down across the yard and out of sight. Phil's mom Jane saw me watching them and said, "men will always be boys," and shook her head.

I asked her what they were doing, and she explained to me that Nathen claimed to be feeding the "Bigfoot" that lived here when in all actuality, he was just feeding the wildlife. She now had my undivided attention. Even Matt came running back up and breathlessly slid into a chair. "Do we really have Bigfoot Nanny"? He asked.

Jane told us that Nathen used to hunt these woods for Deer, Turkey, and wild boar. He saw two of the creatures down by the creek fishing one evening. It scared him so bad he dropped his fresh-killed turkey and ran all the way home. The next morning, his turkey, along with a freshly killed buck, was lying in the back yard. He swears the bigfoot brought it to him. I think one of the neighbors did. Anyway, she said," To make a long story short, he feeds them every night, and they bring him a fresh kill about once a week. Sometimes twice a week". But I think some of our neighbors are just trying to help out an elderly couple, and he's just a foolish old man.

I told Matt to go play and waited for him to leave. I didn't want him to hear anything that might frighten him. I then asked Jane if she had seen one. She told me she had not, but that Nathen swore they came during the wee hours of the morning and took the food he left.

The men were coming back across the yard, so we stopped talking. I could not wait to speak to Phil! We have Bigfoot! I was so excited!

Phil and I declined coffee and cake. We said goodnight and walked back across the yard. I couldn't wait to get him alone and question him. I could tell that he wanted to talk to me too.

After the kids went to bed, we took a cup of coffee and walked out to our picnic table in the backyard. We discussed what was going on with his dad. It seemed he had been doing this for years! He would buy big bags of dog food to add to the food each night. Then he would pour it into big baking pans that he kept just inside the woods. He claimed the food was wholly eaten every night. I wanted to believe, but a big part of me wondered if he wasn't just feeding the wildlife.

I asked Phil what his thoughts on this were. He said, like me, he wanted to believe, but he needed to do something first. When I asked what this something was, he declined to tell me. He just said that I would see what he was talking about tomorrow.

After breakfast, Phil got Matt's game system set up in the living room, and Marlissa curled up on the couch with her tablet.

As I was putting dishes away, Phil came into the kitchen. "Wanna come with me?" he asked. Of course, I did! The curiosity was killing me!

We headed back across the yard to his parent's house. We went down to the area that he and his dad had gone to last night. I immediately saw what Phil was up to. His father had cleared the area where the pans were sitting! The containers were empty this morning. But Phil and I both saw partial prints near the pans. The area wasn't wide enough for there to be full prints on the ground, but we could clearly see the partial ones!

Phil got down on his hands and knees and started clearing the weeds and grass back further to make a more extensive clearing. I immediately dropped to my knees to help. In no time, we had a ten by ten area cleared down to the bare earth. On our way back to the house, we saw the deer lying in the back yard! Neither of us had noticed it coming in. Had they done this while we were working? Phil walked over to the deer. He said the only thing wrong with it was a broken neck. That was strange, I didn't know of any hunters that did this, but I had read that Bigfoot could.

I can't tell you how excited I was!! It only took a couple of days for us to get a full print that we could cast. It was our first time at casting a print, but, I was well pleased with the way it came out.

Phil and I had begun to leave pans of food behind our house as well. But knowing that we had Bigfoot in the area, Phil fenced in our yard for the dogs and for Matt's safety.

Gradually we started hearing the yells and the whoops coming from the woods. Phil and I were fascinated! We were like addicts with a drug, each little thing we got left us longing for more. We both wanted to see one.

We spent endless hours in the woods, waiting and watching. We set up cameras and audio recorders everywhere, still nothing substantial. Nothing we were doing was bringing the results we were wanting. Finally, Phil got an idea, we would gradually move the food pans out into the open. This would have to take some time because it had to be so gradual that they wouldn't notice. A few months later, with still no results, Phil stopped feeding them. Our downfall began.

It began with rocks hitting the house, and us, if we were out in the backyard. The back fence has been torn down many times. The alarms were set off on our cars at night. We have had windows broken out of our homes and vehicles.

The fresh kills no longer show up. I know longer let the kids walk alone to their grandparent's house. Months later, Nathen had a heart attack while out fishing in the creek. Jane had a stroke and no longer talks. I am scared for the kids and us. But Phil still wants that foolproof evidence. He swears that he will eventually get it.

There is no doubt in my mind that they are here. We see the signs daily. I finally started to feed them again, but it hasn't helped. They won't leave us alone now. I watch their dark shadows move in the tree line. I hear their knocks and whoops. What was once fascinating is now terrifying

It feels like the calm before the storm. I wish we had never angered them!

I know that some of you won't believe my story, and that's OK. Thanks to Melissa, I told this story for me. I admitted my faults, I accepted my guilt, and I acknowledged my terror. Believe it if you want to, and take from it what you may. Thank you for reading.

If you enjoyed this book, please consider leaving a review.

Also, you might want to check out some of Melissa's other titles.

1. **Bigfoot Chronicles, A true story**

2. **Bigfoot Chronicles 2, A true story**

3. **Sasquatch, The Native Truth. A true story**

4. **Sasquatch, The Native Truth. Kecleh-Kudleh Mountain A true story**

5. **Sasquatch, The Native Truth. Ravens Return A true story**

6. **The True Haunting of a Paranormal Investigator**

7. **Dog Man, A True Encounter**

8. **Black-Eyed Kids. My Three Months of Hell**. A true story

9. **Family Ties**. Fiction

10. **Female Bigfoot Encounters**. True Stories

11. **Our Paranormal Reality, A True Haunting. Book 1 The Early Years**

12. **Our Paranormal Reality, A True Haunting. Book 2 The Investigation**

13. **Bigfoot, A New Reality. A True Story**

14. **The Birth of a Psychic with Telekinesis. A True Story**

15. **Lifting the Veil on All Things Paranormal, True Stories**

16. **Desolate Mountain, One woman's true story of survival**.

17. The Watcher, A true story.

18. Bigfoot Found me. One man's true encounter with Bigfoot.

19. Goodbye. A true story of an Ouija board experience

20. Sasquatch Travels. Based on a true story

21 Dream House

22. Breast Cancer, Faith, God & Home Free

23. Wood Bugger. One boy's true story of growing up with Bigfoot

24. The Doll.

25. A Week in Bigfoot Territory

Melissa's books can be found online at

Amazon, Barnes and Noble, Books a Million

Wal-Mart and your local
bookstore.

Follow Melissa on,

Her Blog;

http://www.melissageorge.net/

Facebook;

https://www.facebook.com/MelissaGeorgeParanormalAuthor/

Twitter;

https://twitter.com/AuthorMelissaG

Pinterest;

https://www.pinterest.com/melissa6144/

Instagram;

https://www.instagram.com/authormelissageorge/

Get sneak peeks on upcoming books. And enjoy book
giveaways with every new
release!http://melissageorge.net/

About the Author.

Melissa was born and raised in a small town in upstate South Carolina. She first became a well-known Blogger and later decided to take her writing a step further. Her first book, My Paranormal Life, A True Haunting, started out as her own private journal of her family dealing with a dark entity. But it doesn't stop there, Melissa took it even further and let her experiences help her to co-found a paranormal team and a cryptid team. She enjoys being able to reach out and help others. She has made many new friends in both of these fields. Which, in turn, has also led her to help others to have their story told. Melissa realizes first hand that these people have a very passionate and unique story that needs to be heard. In getting these compelling stories out to the public, she hopes it will help further research in both of these fields. Just maybe the individual that shares their story with her may find some closure to their own personal nightmare. Melissa feels honored to be able to bring you true stories of the unexplained.

If you have a story, you would like to see published or just want someone to talk to. I promise you complete anonymity.

Melissageorge143@gmail.com

Printed in Great Britain
by Amazon